To: J

Good to be brothers. You are always in my prayers.

Abundant Blessings
Charles

To: Jim,

Good to be brothers. You are always in my prayers.

Abundant Blessings,
-Nate

What We Believe That Makes Us Different

"A New Thought Journey

Through An Orthodox Land"

By

Charles DeTurk

What We Believe That Makes Us Different – Copyright © 2009 by Charles DeTurk. All rights reserved. Printed in the United States of America. No part of this book may be used or reproduced in any manner whatsoever without written permission except in the case of brief quotations embodied in critical articles and reviews. For information, address Practical Truth, P.O. Box 1763, Decatur, GA 30031, E-mail: revdeturk@yahoo.com

First Edition September 2009
Second Edition December 2009
Third Edition November 2010

© 2009 by Rev. Charles DeTurk
Cover "Sunrise At Tybee" © 2008 by Charles DeTurk
Background "Hunting Island, SC" © 2008 by Charles DeTurk
Back Photograph © 2008 by Charles DeTurk
The quotes from *Let There Be Light: The Seven Keys* by Rocco A. Errico are reprinted by permission of Noohra Foundation, Publishers. Copyright 1994. The quotes from Charles Fillmore's *The Metaphysical Bible Dictionary* are in public domain as Mister Fillmore believed that the Truth should be free to all.

This book is dedicated to my lovely wife, Sherri, long the love of my life on this earthly plane of existence, and the one who is always there to encourage me to be who I am and who I claim to be.

My special thanks to Claire Blehr for going after this manuscript with a hatchet. I have learned a lot from her about grammatically proper writing. I also wish to thank John Strickland, Richard Billings, Thomas Coates, Daniel Perin, George Stone, Kenneth Grosch, Jim Bush and Dan Estes. Your input and comments have all been taken very seriously and I appreciate your time and feedback. And a special thanks to Willowbei Eversole for his pages and pages of commentary. A true Piscean effort. My gratitude also goes to all of the other people who are beyond number and who have encouraged me in this endeavor over the years. I don't know if I ever would have finished it without you. And finally, a special thanks to my wife, Sherri, for the swift kick that she gave me that resulted in me wrapping this journey up so that we can move on to what's next.

Contents

Chapter 1	Introduction	9
Chapter 2	God Is All There Is	35
Chapter 3	God Is All Good	45
Chapter 4	There Is No Evil	55
Chapter 5	We Are One With God	73
Chapter 6	God's Expression Is Infinite	87
Chapter 7	You Are Unique	105
Chapter 8	Ultimate Sin Is Denial Of The Truth	127
Chapter 9	In The Garden Of Eden	151
Chapter 10	You Are The Christ	163
Chapter 11	Our Purpose Is To Be	173
	Ten Statements	188

INTRODUCTION

What We Believe That Makes Us Different

INTRODUCTION

Today, we're where few of us expected to be, even a short time ago. Our reality is altering at an unprecedented rate, forcing us to change and to grow in ways that are sometimes uncomfortable. And yet, in spite of the discomfort, by and large, life is getting better. However, finding our way through the discomfort is not always easy, and particularly when we are bombarded by the viewpoints of others. I would like to dedicate this book to the rediscovery of your own personal independence from the limiting restraints that others, and you yourself, would place upon yourself in an effort to keep yourself from rediscovering the truth about yourself. That truth is that you are a holy singularity. This book is dedicated to apprehending and comprehending that truth about ourselves.

I have been involved with Unity my entire life. This book will therefore be influenced by, and will deal with, that involvement and its impact upon my belief systems. It is true that I know a lot about Unity. That has come as a result of the years of research required for teaching, and a life dedicated to what I think of as the Spirit of Unity's cofounders, Charles and Myrtle Fillmore.

What I know more than anything else about Unity is how little I know. However, in my search to know, I have, I must admit, discovered a number of perceptions which I think are perhaps unique.

Sometimes I'll take an idea or even just a word and follow where it leads me. My preparation for teaching, I have learned, is my life itself. When I know that I will be teaching or writing on a certain topic, then my every available thought and feeling is drawn to an examination of the pending subject.

One of my many mentors was Buckminster (Bucky) Fuller, who, among other things is most renowned for "inventing" the geodesic dome, an incredibly structurally and economically sound way of building where huge clear span edifices can be constructed out of triangles from a minimum of materials through the intelligent use of the mathematics which underlies all structure in the entire universe. One of the ideas that I learned from Bucky is that every event in the universe has a minimum of twelve viewpoints. Twelve different perspectives. Not one truth, but twelve different and unique aspects of truth. Bucky was able to demonstrate this principle with mathematically based models. And I will be sharing the science behind that in this book.

A minimum of twelve different perspectives. What do you suppose would happen if, when two or more people had a difference of "opinion" they stopped, acknowledged that there were, at minimum, at least ten more perspectives on the issue at hand, and that each of those minimum ten perspectives were just as valid as the two positions that they were taking in order to precipitate an argument? And then what if they proceeded to discover and investigate the other viewpoints instead of trying to beat one another into the impossible submission to only one puny viewpoint?

I'd like to share a quote with you from R.D. Laing's book, *The Politics of Experience*. "You experience your experience, and I experience my experience. You cannot experience my experience and I cannot experience your experience. You can only experience your experience of my experience and I can only experience my experience of your experience."

How profound. I first read those words 40 years ago, and I remind myself regularly of their implication. Each of us is absolutely, totally, incredibly unique. In all of the infinity of universe, past, present and future, there is none like you. You are therefore very special.

I want to give you a perspective that I wrote on how incredible your uniqueness is. I call this story, "In A Little Grain of Sand." I first learned about what I'm going to share with you from a column in an entertainment paper in Albuquerque, New Mexico. I've published this article on my website on the Internet, and I'd like to share it with you here, if you'll bear with me.

"In A Little Grain of Sand"

Something extremely interesting happened recently that you might not have heard about. Or, if you did hear about it, the impact of this happening may have escaped you. So I wanted to share it with you. But first, let's go back into the past to an event which just recently had renewed repercussions when it popped up in the media.

In Pisa, Italy (that's right, the home of the leaning tower), on February 15, 1564 (over 400 years ago), just three days before the death of Michelangelo, Galileo Galilei was born. There is much that we could say about this great scientist, but we'll narrow our focus here to a couple of specific points. Galileo was one of the first human beings on this planet to see stars and other celestial bodies (like some of the moons of Jupiter) that could not be seen with the naked eye. He was not the first. The telescope, which allowed him to accomplish this feat, was actually first built in Holland in 1609 when he was already 45 years old. However, Galileo is the first human being to use this new tool to make some very important discoveries of observation that literally shook the culture of his time.

What Galileo discovered, when viewing the "heavens" through his telescopes, confirmed theories and predictions made by Nicolas Copernicus, who had died over two decades before Galileo was born. These discoveries of Galileo created major problems. Up until that time, the Christian church promoted a view of the universe that placed the earth at its center, with everything else revolving around us. This view came from the astronomer Ptolemy, who lived a hundred years after Jesus. Ptolemy got many of his ideas from Hipparchus, a Greek astronomer born in Nicaea about 190 B.C.E. (BC), and who was the first person to accurately measure the distance to the moon. He also created many of the instruments which would be used for the next 17 centuries in what was known as naked eye astronomy.

This concept of the earth as the center of the universe was very important to the church's presentation of reality and its emphasis upon the importance of humanity as God's creation. So when Copernicus proposed that the earth was not the center of the universe, but was, rather, a small player in a much bigger, and sometimes seemingly disorganized, system, the church took offense. Then along came Galileo who used the telescope to prove much of Copernicus's theories to be true. What's more, Galileo, becoming a master craftsman at creating lenses, and then spreading his own telescopes throughout Europe, even had one of his telescopes wind up in the hands of Johan Kepler, a German astronomer who further refined the ideas of Copernicus, to the church's continued consternation.

In 1632, Galileo published, in Italian, Dialogue on the Two Chief World Systems. The pope and the church were doubly angered. First, the pope, Urban VIII, took the book as a personal attack and felt that Galileo had made him out to be a fool. Secondly, publishing in Italian, rather than Latin, allowed not only the learned, but even the general public to read his work. It was quickly translated into many other languages, including Chinese. This affront to the teaching of the church ultimately resulted in Galileo's being brought before the Inquisition the following year on charges of heresy.

Galileo was forced by the church to recant his views. Some might wonder why he would do this. Perhaps, at the ripe old age of 69 he had thoughts of the Italian philosopher Giordano Bruno, who some 30 years earlier was burned alive at the stake by the Inquisition for professing such heresy as the infinity of space and the motion of the earth. Whatever the reason, Galileo recanted his claims and the church's incorrect beliefs continued. Those beliefs were so strong that Harvard University, in the year of its founding, 1636, remained firmly committed to Ptolemaic theory.

In 1835, after 200 years, Galileo's Dialogue was finally removed from the Roman Catholic Index of prohibited books. Then, in 1965, on a visit to Pisa, Pope Paul VI, spoke highly of Galileo. Finally, just before the end of the 20th Century, the Catholic Church officially reversed itself upon Galileo, essentially pardoning him, and thereby finally admitting that he was right in the first place and had been all along. And it only took a little over 350 years for them to acknowledge his contribution to human knowledge.

Now, with that as a perspective, let's take a look at what happened just the other day (give or take a few years). The quest for observing the universe took a giant step with the placing in orbit of the Hubble Space Telescope. Few know that this telescope was named for Edwin Powell Hubble, of the Palomar Observatory, who helped discover in the 1920's that there were other galaxies in the universe besides our own Milky Way galaxy. During the next 80 years, we have discovered that there are literally billions of galaxies, and, furthermore, that on the average, each of those galaxies contains over a billion stars. That's over a billion billion stars similar to our sun.

Buckminster Fuller used to point out that universe is defined as the sum total of humanity's combined experience. Therefore, every time we are able to "see" further into space, our universe expands that distance in all directions, for that becomes a possible part of our experience. So we had arrived at a place in the 1990's where, due to the Hubble Telescope, our ability to see into space had increased to a radius of something like 11 billion light years. That means that we had been able to observe at least one source of radiating energy at least 11 billion light years from earth. To grasp the gravity of this reality, light travels at 86,282 miles per second. Therefore, in a year it travels 60 seconds * 60 minutes * 24 hours * 365 days * 86,282 miles = 2 (trillion), 722 (billion), 852 (million), 843 (thousand), 200 miles. That's almost 2 3/4 trillion miles. Then we have to multiply that by 11 billion years, which equals some 29,951,381,275,200,000,000,000 miles. That's almost 30 sextillion miles, or a number that's damn near impossible for most people to even comprehend; 30 followed by 21 zeroes. That means that the radiation that we detected from that 11 billion light year heavenly body began its 30 sextillion mile journey to be intercepted by our observation with Hubble 11 billion years ago. But that's just in one direction. Think now of a sphere with a radius of 11 billion light years. That's beyond huge. And that's where we consciously are because of Hubble's being in orbit.

But that's nothing but a drop in the bucket compared to what happens next. Someone got the bright idea of taking the Hubble Space Telescope and pointing it at what was generally considered to be "empty space." If we look up in the sky at night when we're away from the city, we notice that there are some parts of the sky which seem to be devoid of stars. So it has been even with the strongest of telescopes. There are just some places where there appears to be nothing, or close to it. So they decided to point Hubble at some of this "empty space" and see if there might be something there.

Now, just how much empty space are we talking about? Well, to give you a real clear idea, I want you to extend your arm right now as far as you can toward the sky. Now, imagine that you are holding a grain of sand between your thumb and forefinger. They pointed the Hubble telescope toward a piece of empty space that can be obscured by that tiny grain of sand that you are holding at arm's length. All of the space behind a grain of sand. And guess what they saw? Hidden in that tiny grain of sand of supposedly empty space they found over 3,000 galaxies. At our predetermined average of 1 billion stars in a galaxy, they discovered 3,000,000,000,000 (3 trillion) stars hidden in a piece of empty space the size of a grain of sand.

We have now moved into areas of perception which are practically beyond our current ability to comprehend. How many grains of sand would it take to obscure our entire view of space? And each grain containing over 3 trillion suns. "What a piece of work is man," Shakespeare proclaimed. True, or not?

Well, when considering our ability to discover, comprehend, and contemplate the vastness of the universe in which we thrive, Shakespeare was spot on. For an additional perspective upon our thoughts here, I'd like to share with you some thoughts from James A. Michener's book, Space. This was not, incidentally, in the television series based loosely on the book. The character here, Stanley Mott, is a rocket scientist, who, during the early days of our space program, feeling overwhelmed by some of the problems in his life, seeks a bit of solitude, some time to become still and regroup his energies.

Stanley Mott, striving to attain some sense of what the universe was, sat perfectly still on the bank of the Tennessee River, south of Huntsville, Alabama. Keeping arms and legs motionless, he endeavored to move not even his eyes, for he wished to experience the sensation of a body at complete rest, and at last he achieved this. He was as still as a human being could be; indeed, he might as well be dead except for the inescapable functioning of autonomic systems like breathing and heart beating.

"I am motionless," he said to himself at last, and he kept this posture for ten minutes, thinking of nothing. Then his brain insisted, recalling data he had memorized at Cal Tech:

"But at this moment I'm sitting on a piece of Earth at 34 degrees 30 minutes North, which means I'm spinning west to east at a rate of about 860 miles an hour. At the equator, because of the larger bulge, 1,040 miles an hour. At the same time, my Earth is moving through its orbit around the Sun at 66,661 miles an hour, and my Sun is carrying itself and its planets toward the star Vega at something like 31,000 miles an hour.

"Our Sun and Vega move around the Galaxy at the blinding speed of 700,000 miles per hour, and the Galaxy itself rotates at 559,350 miles an hour.

"And that's not all. Our Galaxy moves in relation to all other galaxies as they rush through the

universe at a speed of better than 1,000,000 miles an hour.

"So when I sit here absolutely still I'm moving in six wildly different directions at an accumulated speed of ..... maybe two and a half million miles an hour. So I can never be motionless. I'm traveling always at speeds which are incomprehensible. And it's all happening in real time."

He considered these demonstrable facts for some moments, then concluded:

"And perhaps the universe itself is hurtling toward some undefined destination at a speed which could hardly be stated, perhaps to clear our space for a better universe which will supplant us, while we rush off to some new adventure."

When he rose and felt his limbs moving only inches, he thought: "What a trivial journey we make. Inches under our own power, two and a half million miles with the universe. But ours is the journey that counts. Our slow inching along to understanding and control." When he headed back to his car, he calculated that he was walking at a rate of perhaps 2.3 miles an hour, hardly worth noting in comparison to the speeds he had been dealing with: "And yet, for millions of years of our existence," he thought, "that's about the best we could do. It got us where we are, and that's not trivial."

What we could say is that what we do is of little relevance, yet what we accomplish is spectacular. It's all in our perspective. What phenomenal truth awaits us in a little grain of sand! This recent discovery is one that further shakes the fundamental foundations of the church, though it only adds to the teachings of the church's original founder. For in a universe so vast and so grand, the very fact that we can consciously participate as a part of that universe, to interact with it, to discover its principles, and to turn those principles into creations that ensure the ongoing development of our species, to realize that just as the universe is vast beyond our comprehension and exquisitely expansive, likewise, so are we. And that is truly awareness of a spiritual sort.

The incredible vastness of the universe in which we live is beautiful beyond description. It should give us all pause when weighing the "important" events in our everyday lives against the exquisite background in which we live. Contemplating this expanded reality in which we find ourselves could very well bring us closer together, through the realization that we might be better off if we don't segregate ourselves into unique aloneness. Through discoveries such as this, the inhabitants of this planet are being brought together into an awareness of the unity which we share with one another as the crew of this magnificent spaceship upon which we all live. It is therefore time to rethink the procedures and the structures and the systems which we have relied upon for centuries, all of those systems which got us to where we are, and to ask ourselves if it is not time for some major changes in our focus and in our direction.

I am dedicated to revealing new perspectives which might well lead us to new procedures and beliefs and systems that will greatly enhance life as we know it. We are here looking for answers. We were designed to be curious. For too long, the results of that curiosity have been systematically stifled, as in the case of Galileo. Many of our most outspoken "leaders" today speak of paradigm shifts, radical changes in consciousness, yet the paradigms which many profess are often very simple and elementary. I see paradigm shifts, alterations in our view of reality, that are earth shaking.

I believe it was Alfred North Whitehead who said that "all major changes in civilization essentially all but destroy the cultures in which they are discovered." I would further point out that if those changes are stifled, then the culture in question withers away just the same. So I cast my vote for expansive growth and change.

For these thoughts, I thank Norma Jean Thompson of the "Albuquerque Alibi," for first making me aware of the Hubble grain of sand. To Isaac Asimov, I'm always indebted for the vast collection of knowledge which he compiled during his lifetime, specifically his marvelous, Asimov's Biographical Encyclopedia of Science & Technology. I'm grateful to Bucky Fuller for instilling in me the desire for discovery and the constant belief in the ultimate goodness of humanity. My thanks go to James Michener for being able to place exciting concepts in an enjoyable context of learning. And, of course, my overwhelming gratitude to all of the people throughout our species' existence, who have wondered and who have persevered in following the inner leading to wherever that wonder will take them.

Early in my experience in Unity I was fortunate to grasp the direction in which Charles Fillmore was headed in his discovery of the principles and practices which evolved into what we call Unity. His spiritual realization was an ongoing process of continual discovery and growth. And I took that direction of his as a personal principle of action in my own life.

Let me share with you how Unity defines Papa Charlie's approach to discerning the truth about ourselves. This is taken from the frontispiece of Charles' magnum opus:

The Metaphysical Bible Dictionary was compiled and published in 1931. It is one of the basic books containing Charles Fillmore's inspired thinking and teaching, which we regard as a vital part of our spiritual heritage.

Charles Fillmore was an innovative thinker, a pioneer in metaphysical thought at a time when most religious thought in America was entirely orthodox. He was a lifelong advocate of the open, inquiring mind, and he took pride in keeping abreast of the latest scientific and educational discoveries and theories. Many years ago he wrote, "what you think today may not be the measure of your thought tomorrow;" and it seems likely that were he to compile this book today, he might use different metaphors, different scientific references, and so on.

Truth is changeless. Those who knew Charles Fillmore best believe that he would like to be able to rephrase some of his observations for today's readers, thus giving them the added effectiveness of contemporary thought. But the ideas themselves - the core of Charles Fillmore's writing - are as timeless now (and will be tomorrow) as when they were first published.

The "open, inquiring mind." It's like when I first met Buckminster Fuller and I asked him what he would recommend that I do with my life. I was wondering whether or not I should go back to school. He response was simple and to the point. "Life!" he said.

"Life itself is the greatest teacher and will give you all that you seek." But, in seeking life, one must, of course, also deal with the others out there. And that can present a new layer of complexity.

When I was growing up in Atlanta several decades ago, I remember one Sunday morning my younger brother, Larry, and I hearing a Baptist minister on the radio say, in a slow southern preacher's drawl, "The devil is walkin' the streets of Atlanta." With eyes wide open, we both looked around expectantly. Then the preacher went on to say, "And his name is Unity." Well, this time we moved a bit away from one another as we looked one at the other, and again looked around us. Needless to say, we were shocked. Having grown up in Unity, we wondered how it could be that others would think of our teachings and our beliefs as being the work of the devil.

As my life progressed, I was going to discover a long line of people who would question and even condemn my beliefs. As a result, for many years I was very cautious about sharing what I believed, and how I truly felt, with anyone other than my very close friends and some, but not all, of my family members. To open up and to be honest with others seemed sometimes to be nothing more than an invitation to attacks that were intimidating, if not, in fact, at times, quite vicious.

In my late teens, my mother, Bette DeTurk, became an Ordained Unity Minister. Needless to say, my brother, Larry, and I were a large and important part of her ministry. I remember occasionally accompanying her to various Christian bookstores to buy books, paper, or other supplies, and occasionally, while browsing around, I would happen upon books that professed to enlighten one to the danger of "cults". I still remember my initial shock to discover that Unity was listed in many of these books as a cult. "Why would anyone say that about us?" I wondered.

Upon perusing the books in question I would find them making various claims about what Unity supposedly believed. With each claim that they made, however, I would respond, "that's right," and wonder why they objected to that belief. Every accusatory claim they made seemed to regard something that naturally made perfect sense to me, contrary to their criticism. Of course, sometimes they would take something and twist it out of context, but by and large the bottom line seemed to be that we saw the thing differently and they claimed that I was wrong.

I remember once receiving a series of emails from a number of self-proclaimed "Unitics" in response to a conservative, fundamentalist Christian posting on their Internet discussion board. The post apparently opened old wounds from past religious experiences for several of the board's participants. One person so objected to the posting that they withdrew from further involvement with the board. Another person requested that the "owner" of the "discussion board" take steps to remove this "invader." It's obvious that many people have beliefs that are still in a fragile state of growth and development, and they can easily feel overwhelmed by those who "act" as if they know more. And, unfortunately, there are plenty of religious activists out there in the world who over-zealously tromp haphazardly upon the beliefs of others while trying to heavy-handedly peddle their own narrow-minded set of beliefs.

It's interesting to note, however, that on a couple of Internet discussion boards which I have followed, the greatest amount of participation seems to occur when someone enters the discussion in a predatory way, appearing to trample on the sensibility of others. Then everyone gets involved by jumping in and arguing between condemning the offender for offending others, or protecting the offender's right to be offensive. Why can't we get as excited about what we believe as we can about what we don't believe? It's just like the fact that many people listen to talk radio programs in spite of the fact that they find the content to be extremely objectionable. I myself have caught myself riding down the highway arguing with a radio talk show host's comments without even asking myself why it is that I am bothering to listen to them if I find their viewpoints so objectionable.

It reminds me of the time I snuck a mother and her four grown daughters into a theater to view the, then popular, extremely x-rated movie, "Deep Throat." All five of these women stood in the back of the theater saying, "Oh, that's terrible," "How could anyone do that," "This is disgusting," and so on. But the fact of the matter is that they wouldn't leave the theater. They chose, instead, to remain and to appear to continue to be offended by what they were seeing on the screen. "I can't stand watching this," they would say, as they continued to watch voyeuristically.

I remember one Sunday, when we attended Dr. Barbara King's Hillside Chapel and Truth Center in Atlanta, Georgia, to hear Dr. Rocco Errico preach. For those who know of Dr. Errico's work, you might wonder why I used the word "preach" instead of "teach." It's because that's what happens when Dr. Errico speaks at Dr. King's church on Sunday morning. He gets on fire with the truth of the love of God indwelling and flowing through each of us and that presence of God expresses through him as a glorious shower of exquisite energy. And you just have to call it preaching. Of course, that should come as no surprise, for Dr. King's work at Hillside is a phenomenally open expression of the beauty and the energy of the principles of truth.

On that morning, however, surrounded by 800 people who were caught up in the spirit of Spirit expressing through Dr. Errico, a look around the room revealed an occasional soul who showed no outer manifestation of the joyous love that was expressing through every aspect of that entire service. And it reminded me of a time when I too was still afraid to let the joy of the Christ within express through me. I was afraid of what the world might think if I should let them know who I really thought I was, if I acted as I really felt led to act. In other words, I was living a life of feeling intimidated by others. Sound familiar?

Over the years, as I have grown older, not knowing just how to respond to the questions that some people have put to me has been bothersome, to say the least. At times, it has made me feel very incompetent and insecure. Then, one day, I decided to draw the line and begin to figure out what I believed. It didn't turn out to be anything very elaborate, just a few words and phrases on a 3 x 5 card. I was prompted to do this as a result of a profound experience at a Carlos Santana concert in the Paolo Soleri Amphitheater at the Indian School in Santa Fe, New Mexico. The title of Carlos' latest album at the time was "Spirits Dancing In The Flesh." I liked that idea and the show that night was a truly magic time of love, peace, and joy.

So, I got myself a card that would fit in my pocket and I wrote a short list of basic concepts that I felt I believed in. It was sort of like a private code because only I fully understood what each statement meant, for each was based upon my own personal beliefs and experiences. It looked like this:

About God
Remember: Spirits all around you, dancin' in the flesh.
Remember: I Am that I Am.
Remember: Always has been, is now, and always will be.
Remember: Christ in you, your hope of glory.
Remember: Parallel Universes.
Remember: Goldsmith's "Letter to Sam"

Those few words were a comfort and a security to me in times when I felt that I might be losing my way. Quickly reading over them reminded me of all that each statement represented to me. Now some people might say, "If you believe it, why do you have to remind yourself." But most people understand what I'm saying here. Life is a constant renewing process and sometimes we let our awareness slip back into old belief patterns and our newfound perspectives appear to begin to dissolve before our very eyes. I often advise people that they need to realize that every day when they awake, it's like starting all over, again. It's not enough to think that one has "made it" and no longer needs to do anything. Although this book is not about those six statements, I feel that I should expound upon them briefly so that the reader will know why they were meaningful for me.

Spirits all around you, dancin' in the flesh. This could either be taken as "There are spirits all around you" or that "Spirit is all around you." Either way, it's dancing in the flesh. The flesh is the world that we presently inhabit, and that habitation is like a dance. Each of us has our own dance. Sometimes our dance merges with the dance of others; other times we may seem to dance alone. But all in all, we are living in an extraordinary ballet. We would all probably be a lot better off if we realized that we are dancing and we began to dance with a more deliberate passion.

I Am that I Am. This is the name that God gave to Moses on Mount Sinai when Moses asked whom he should say sent him. Those five words puzzled me for much of my life, for if you emphasize a different word each time you say that phrase (name), the meaning seems to be a little bit different. In a nutshell, however, it had come to mean to me that "God is" and "I am" and that the I that I am is God in expression.

Always has been, is now, and always will be. This represents the infinite eternality of all that is, and therefore, the eternity of God and all of God's creation. Our concept of reality is merely a few frames in the infinite ongoing movie of existence.

Christ in you, your hope of glory. Those words are from Paul's letter to the Colossians. For all of the sometimes bizarre stuff that Paul may have said, occasionally he was spot on. I believe that this was one of those times. Genesis says that God created man in God's image and after God's likeness. I believe that the term for that divine creation is Christ. And that divine perfection of the Christ is at the core of each and every one of us. That includes every single one of us, whether we are expressing it well or not. There can be no hope beyond expressing the divinity that we are.

Parallel Universes. Ah, this comes from Dr. Fred Alan Wolf. Fred helped me to see the reality in which we live from whole new perspectives. Radical perspectives. He says, in his book, *Parallel Universes*, that in order for quantum physics to "work," that all possibilities have to exist. That's not that they must "possibly exist," but that they must "exist," period. And therefore, in order for that to happen, there must be an infinite number of parallel universes. The first time that the awareness of what this thought meant impacted upon my brain, I was driving down an interstate in New Mexico through the Sandia Indian Reservation. The realization of what parallel universes meant shocked me so much that I almost ran off the highway.

And finally, **Goldsmith's *Letter to Sam*.** Joel Goldsmith, western mystic, wrote a letter to his son, Sam, when Sam went off to college. In a nutshell, what the letter said was that when one knows the truth, then one can accept and flow with all circumstances, for knowing the truth gives one the knowledge of what underlies all circumstance. Seeing the oneness that is beyond the separation of appearance allows one to avoid viewing life with an overly critical eye and brings harmony and a unity to our life experience.

Those six phrases helped me to keep going for several years, until my next big breakthrough in understanding. Whenever I was confronted by religious combatants, I could find solace in the "About God" statements that I carried with me in my shirt pocket. Rest assured, they didn't inspire me sufficiently to speak up as to my own beliefs, but they comforted me sufficiently that the slings and arrows of religious zealots ceased to faze me as much.

When I became an ordained minister, I began to perform a lot of weddings. Very few of the people that I officiated for were folks that I knew before they approached me, usually through a small ad that I had run somewhere. I very quickly came to enjoy not only the wedding ceremony, but also the reception that followed. It was during these receptions that I often met new people who would ask me about what "church" I was with and what it is that I believe. Over time I began to develop some comfortable "pat" answers that gave others the impression that they understood what my religious beliefs were, but I learned much from these spontaneous conversations.

Then, one day, a self-styled agent for converting the world to a narrow Christian viewpoint once again confronted me. I refer to this individual as "Brandon the banker" because his name was Brandon, and he was a teller in the bank that I used at that time. The whole episode started out innocent enough. When Brandon noticed that my deposit slip said Practical Truth Ministry, he asked me if I was a minister and just what I believed. One question led to another until his questions began to sound more like accusations.

After enduring several minutes of his assault of "questions" about my "personal savior" and about whether or not I had been "washed in the blood" and had experienced "personal redemption," I refused to speak with Brandon any further. It seemed to me that Brandon's persistent questions had little relevance to the truth of allowing the Christ to express in our lives.

As I left the bank that day, I found myself feeling quite disturbed about what had just transpired. I asked myself why it was that the "Brandons" of the world still upset me so, for I did walk out of the bank inwardly fuming, just as I would occasionally boil when listening to talk radio. The answer to my question was one that I had been aware of for a long time, yet hadn't known how to rectify. My faith in my own belief system wasn't as strong as it needed to be. With a strong faith and a firm belief, what others think and say about one's convictions is irrelevant. I felt bothered by their questions because I didn't feel confident about what I believed.

It became obvious to me that the "About God" card that I had created five years earlier needed an expansive overhaul. My experience with Brandon the banker told me that I needed to once again become firmer in my convictions. Of course to do that required that I identify those self same convictions. So I asked myself, "What is it that you believe that makes you so different that others find cause to criticize your beliefs?"

"Well," I responded, "first, I believe that God is all there is." That statement right there can get some pretty interesting discussions started. Anyway, in no time at all I had written down ten interconnected statements that I felt identify what I believe that are in a harmony with the teachings of Unity that I had been raised upon. Those statements clearly identify areas that sometimes light the fires of disapproval amongst our more fundamentalist friends and acquaintances.

Those ten statements became an eleven-session series of lessons entitled "What We Believe That Makes Us Different." I have taught it many times and have even published the notes from one of those eleven-week sessions on a now-defunct website, Practical Truth Ministry, and posted them on my Practical Truth weblog (http://practicaltruth.blogspot.com).

In the coming chapters, I will share with you my thoughts on these ten points in hopes that it might give you some added insight into your own set of beliefs. We'll take one statement at a time. If you're looking for the ten statements themselves, you will find them in the final chapter.

If you are one of those "bottom line" kinds of people, you can jump to the end of the book and get a synopsis of what this is all about. But I hope that you won't do that, for I have a lot of interesting insight to share with you that expounds upon these points through a number of different perspectives. In fact, I'm so confident in the value of what you will find in this book that I will make you this assurance: I guarantee that you will be exposed to ideas and perspectives that you have never before considered. I can make that guarantee because much of what is in this book revealed itself to me through individual meditation, personal, original thoughts, and unique experience.

One might question my right to say what Unity believes. Yet, who would better know what Unity means to me than I, myself? And the same is true of you. God has created each of us to have dominion over all of the world. That doesn't mean to "rule" the world as an autocrat. What it means is that we are each of us responsible for determining the kind of world, or reality, in which we live. We determine what beliefs will guide us through life. We make our own heaven and our own hell. We are the creators of our own reality. And although I may speak "of" Unity, I do not pretend to speak "for" Unity. And Unity might not be a right fit for you, but nevertheless you may very well find the ideas contained within this book to be of value to you.

You will find references to Unity throughout this book and quotes from Unity's co-founder, Charles Fillmore. When I first wrote the book, I quoted quite extensively from Charles' book, *Metaphysical Bible Dictionary (MBD)*. I did this because I think that somebody needs to do it. It is a marvelously profound book and yet one seldom hears anyone referring to it, and quoting more than a few words. Its title is very clear. It is a dictionary of biblical terms as seen from a metaphysical perspective. After running this book you hold in your hands, or see on your screen, by a dozen or so folk for editing input, I have decided to axe most of the *MBD* quotes. I recommend that the reader read the areas in the *MBD* that I reference, but I have removed the bulk of them for easier book flow.

The reader also needs to know that when I use a quote, it's sometimes quite lengthy. I don't like grabbing "sound bites" or using little snippets to construct a picture. I have learned from my own experience as a minister, preparing for a class or to give a talk, that the "whole context" adds depth and a fuller understanding to what we're talking about. I have tried, however, to keep long quotes to a minimum.

This book was originally a series of classes and talks and email, blog and web postings. In that context, I wanted to make certain that I was presenting a full picture at the moment rather than relying on listeners to remember later to "check my sources." For this very same reason, I have been known, on occasion, to present a Sunday morning talk that was 100% quotation.

The first of these occasions, as I recall, had to do with the so-called "Sermon On The Mount." Everyone has heard parts of that "sermon." And if one has read the Bible, then one has read that entire sermon. But in preparation for speaking about it, I realized that I've never heard of anyone "giving" this sermon, other than Jesus. So, the next Sunday I gave, "read," the "Sermon On The Mount" right out of the Bible. It actually makes for a very profound talk.

This is something I also did with one of my mother's Sunday talks. It was so good that I merely presented it as she had, word for word. No need to embellish. My ego doesn't require the total spotlight; it's easy enough to be the messenger.

One other time that this happened was quite extensive. I was working on preparing to speak on Dr. H. Emilie Cady's wonderful book, "Lessons In Truth." I've read the book many times. I have answered all of the questions at the end of each chapter. I even had my written answers graded by Unity professionals at Unity School Of Christianity. And I have long taught many of the principles found in that wonderful tome. But this time, I was once again moved by the incredible beauty of what was written.

I realized that most people have not read "Lessons In Truth." Fewer still have attended an entire series of classes based upon the book. Even fewer have actually answered all of the questions that the book presents. And even fewer still have had their answers examined and graded by others. So why, I thought, would I want to begin to present my perspective upon something that so few people really knew very much about in the first place? Therefore, for the next ten Sundays I read (presented) a different chapter from the book, "Lessons In Truth," each week. (Understand that when I "give/read" someone else's work, I make certain that they receive the full credit and that it is understood that I am merely acting as an instrument of presentation.)

Now, why is this book called "What We Believe…" instead of "What I Believe…"? It's very simple, because I am not the only one who believes these things. There are many others who see reality from these, or very similar, perspectives. "We" doesn't refer to any one group or organization. I am not a spokesperson for anyone other than myself. However, I know that there are those, like me, out there who would welcome someone standing up and saying, "This is what I believe." "This is what we believe." Those who constitute the "we" know who they are and that is sufficient.

These ten statements are not cut in stone. They are not the last word. They are merely an expression of my own awareness at the time they were put together. And I wanted to share it with you because I thought you might be interested. Each of the following chapters expounds upon one of these ten statements.

Because I am still in the process of growing, there is another book in the works even as I type these words. It promises to be a real barnburner.

Please know that you are as blessed as you allow yourself to be. Enjoy life! It's a blast!

GOD IS ALL THERE IS

God is all there is; absolute, total, without exception.

GOD IS ALL THERE IS

Even though I grew up in Unity, it took me close to 50 years to finally get a sufficient handle on what it was that I myself really believed so that I was confident enough to openly share those beliefs with others. Oh, I have shared my beliefs all of my life, but not with that inner confidence which now sustains me. And over the years I have talked with thousands of people who have experienced that same kind of hesitancy at sharing their beliefs, or those of Unity or New Thought, with others because they might not yet have that quiet inner assurance which banishes all fear.

Then, in the final decade of the 20th Century, I had an experience that shocked me into confronting my beliefs. Five years later, I was forced once again, on a new level, to come to terms with my deeper faith and understanding. The result of that experience was 10 statements that I wrote down for myself, delineating what I felt I believed that sometimes caused others to question those very beliefs. I then titled those statements "What We Believe That Makes Us Different."

Since that time, I have had people question me about why I talk about differences. But, if you read the statements, you quickly realize that I'm not talking about differences. I'm not talking about exclusion, but rather inclusion, for these beliefs are all inclusive and not that different from the underlying beliefs of all great spiritual teaching. So those who criticize my speaking of differences are merely making their judgment on the "title" of the statements rather than upon the content of the statements themselves. It's called "judging by appearances," and I deliberately used that title to catch people off guard.

Then there are people who state that I have no right to state what Unity believes. But nowhere in the statements do I ever claim that this is what Unity believes. Although I quote extensively from Charles Fillmore, it is not my intention to claim to be a spokesperson for Unity. I am merely speaking from the perspective of someone who has grown up in Unity and am reporting upon how that has impacted upon my own thinking and feeling. This book, therefore, is all based upon what "we" believe. And the "we" of whom I speak refers to those who share in these beliefs, whoever you may be and wherever you may be, whether we've met or not.

I grew up in Unity. I am, therefore, a product of Unity's perspective, and what I believe has been influenced by my lifelong Unity experience. This doesn't mean that I'm a Unity automaton. It merely refers to the fact that Unity and its basic principles played a very important role in my upbringing. Although there are those who claim that I have no right to speak for Unity, not one person has ever been able to point out anything in these statements that is not in alignment with Unity's teachings.

But, because I have had a lifelong connection to the Unity movement, I should probably give my perspective upon Unity and the movement that embraces it. Often, when I am officiating at a wedding, someone will come up to me after the service and say something like, "where is your church," or "what church are you affiliated with?" Over time, I developed a basic answer that quickly furnished enough information to satisfy the questioner that they had gotten an answer to their question.

Here's how it goes: "I grew up in Unity. Are you familiar with Unity? Well, Unity is part of what is sometimes referred to as the New Thought Movement. It got its start in the late 1800's through the spiritual experiences of a Midwest couple who found healing through prayer, and it has roots similar to those of Religious Science and Christian Science. The 'New Thought' that sparked this movement is referring to a statement by Ralph Waldo Emerson, when he spoke of "this new thought" that an individual human being ought to be able to communicate directly with God without having to go through an intermediary. So, in an effort to achieve that personal spiritual experience, Unity is an attempt to return to first century Christianity, to the teachings of Jesus before they became all doctrinized, dogmatized, and ritualized, and then to figure out scientifically how contemporary people can apply those simple, yet profound, teachings to their lives. Unity, therefore, is a modern Christian-based set of practical spiritual teachings. Unity's ongoing strength is founded in prayer, and Unity's headquarters has had people praying continuously 24/7 for over a century."

So, does this mean that what I'm sharing with you is what Unity teaches? No! These statements are specifically titled, "What WE Believe ..." Again, that's me and whomever. You see, the whole of existence is nothing more than perspective. The reality in which you live is absolutely, totally, unique. There is no one else in all of the world who sees the world exactly as you do. There is no one else who has the experiences that you do. There never has been and there never will be. You are exquisitely unique and we'll deal with that uniqueness in the chapters to come. Suffice it for now to simply realize that each of us has a unique perspective, and I've chosen to share mine with whoever is interested because I've found a lot of peace and joy and satisfaction in these beliefs and I want to share that good with others who are open to checking it out.

Although Unity has had a tremendous influence upon my view of reality, it was from Unity that I learned to seek to continue to grow in my understanding of the principles of the universe. My friend, Bucky Fuller, used to say, "Human beings are born naked and ignorant." And, he went on to point out that we have an innate, unlimited curiosity that lasts us a lifetime. We will discover in the course of this book how extremely important that curiosity is to creating the scenario from which we develop our view of reality. And it is that God-given curiosity that has inspired me to build upon the foundation that Unity created for me.

We begin, therefore, with the statement: **God is all there is; absolute, total, without exception.** In the second chapter of Deepak Chopra's book, *Creating Affluence,* he discusses what he calls the "A to Z Steps To Creating Affluence." The letter "A stands for all possibilities, absolute, authority, affluence, and abundance." He goes on to say, "the true nature of our ground state and that of the universe is that it is a field of all possibilities. In our most primordial form, we are a field of all possibilities." This, friends, is what we're talking about when we think of God as being "all there is." All means absolute, and that absolute is the ultimate authority from which springs an unlimited affluence and endless abundance of possibilities.

It is absolutely essential that we begin with this realization of the allness of God. Bucky Fuller used to say that whenever he approached discovering the solution to a problem, that he would begin with total universe and throw out all of the nonessentials. This total universe is what we are talking about here. All means everything. Now that is very difficult for some people to accept for they see so many unGodlike things in their world of experience. And we will be talking about that in the chapters to come. For now, however, we need to understand that as a starting place we begin with a belief in the absolute allness of God.

What is God? Well, God is different things to different people. That's because each of us is, as I've already said, incredibly unique, with our own individual perspective upon this experience that we blithely call reality. This is one of the reasons that God is all there is, that God is infinite, because God must have an unlimited number of appearances to accommodate for the unique perspectives of the infinite unfolding of universe.

The fact of the matter is, we don't know what God is. We don't even know that God is sufficiently real enough that we can prove it to just one other single human being. That's because our perspective of total universe is just that, a single and unique perspective. It is not the total infinity of universe. Later we'll examine some of that infinity. But for now, suffice it to say that we do not have infinite awareness. Our awareness is extremely limited. And yet, within that awareness are some experiences that, if we take the time to listen to them, to feel them, imply to us that there is something greater than us.

There is an order that is obvious in our universe of experience. That order implies a deliberateness that must have a source. What's more, it is obvious that simple systems have an innate drive to evolve. I mean, look at yourself. Look at your physical body. Your body began from a single cell that replicated itself and, following internally coded DNA instructions, grew into the physical you that you are today. How splendidly exquisite. How incredible. How miraculous. And, along the way, coexistent with the evolution of your physical being, your brain came into an incredible beingness of awareness and consciousness. And, not to take away from your parents and the others who love you, you did 99% of this growing on your own. And that growth was all accomplished without an obvious operations manual. Of course the physical operations manual is our DNA; a little microscopic double helix twist of proteins containing the unique blueprint for the structure that houses the you that you present yourself to be.

Now, with that sense of awe over your own creation, think about the rest of the universe. How vast, how amazing, how orderly in a seemingly chaotic way, is the universe of experience in which we appear to exist. Just as you developed consciousness in your growth and evolution from a single cell to the person that you are today, doesn't it make sense that the universe itself would also contain consciousness that has also evolved with time? I can't convince you or anyone of the existence of God, but I can say this: the existence of God only makes sense. In addition, it feels right. And I trust that. I trust what makes sense and what feels right.

So when we say that God is all there is, what we are also saying, as a direct corollary, is that everything that is, is God. Actually the word "God" is a terrible word to use because it has a different meaning for everyone. So we point out here that we define God as everything that is. Therefore, God, by that definition, becomes all that is. In the next chapter we'll take a deeper look into just what that "is that God is," is.

The allness that God is, is infinite. That last term is one that we often use without giving it the thought that it deserves. When we think about it, part of the definition inherent in the word "infinite" is that it is beyond our ability to comprehend. Someone recently told me that when they think about the infinity of time, that it is easier to accept the infinity of the future than it is to comprehend the infinity of the past.

Because human beings are physical beings, functioning in what we think of as a physical universe, we are largely driven in our perception of what we think of as reality by the information reported to us by our physical senses. Most often, this means sight, sound, taste, touch, and smell. In other words, it is any way in which we perceive, or are otherwise aware of, the appearance of physical phenomena around us. Due to the overwhelming infinity of the phenomena of physical universe, our awareness of the physical aspects of our reality of experience far outweighs the other aspects of our experiential existence.

So we tend to perceive all of reality from the limited perspective of mere physical reality. And because physical reality has its own set of rules and principles, we therefore tend to apply those same rules and principles to all of the rest of the reality perceived by our consciousness. An example of this is "beginnings and endings." In physical experience, everything has an apparent beginning and an apparent ending. And we've become so used to that perception that the comprehension of infinity seems beyond our ability to mentally process. We have therefore made our apparent inability to comprehend infinity another concept that is based upon the physical rules, rather than entertaining the possibility that the comprehension of infinity might be possible, but through other modes of perception than those we are accustomed to.

Are these modes of perception that humanity has yet to develop? Perhaps not. J. Robert Oppenheimer, the "father of the atom bomb," is quoted as saying, "there are children, walking the streets today, who can solve some of my most difficult physics problems because they still have modes of perception that I lost long ago." It is therefore our conditioning that perhaps limits our perspective rather than the idea that limitation is innate in our perception itself.

So, simply stated, God is all there is. Period ∞.

GOD IS ALL GOOD

God is all good.

GOD IS ALL GOOD

So we begin with the realization that God is all there is. Looking at the statement from a different perspective, consider everything that possibly is, past, present, future, and absolutely everywhere upon every level of expression, visible and invisible, known and unknown. Add it all together and we call that God, for want of a better word. And we therefore say that God is all there is. Why this is important is that it implies that there is a oneness underlying and connecting everything that is.

Next, we believe that **God is all good.** Now, this is not "good" in the sense of "good and evil." This is "good" rather in the sense of wholeness, balance, and unity. Why is it that God is all good? It can't be just because God is all there is, can it? Well, yes it can. We've all heard the old saying, "Nothing is either good or bad, but thinking makes it so." That statement is truer than we may choose to realize.

In the 1960's and 70's there was an entertainer named Biff Rose. Biffie once said, "Being good implies being bad. Being myself is beyond either good or bad." It is beyond those concepts of good and bad that we are talking about when we say that God is all good.

The Sufi poet Rumi was telling us the same thing when he said, "Out beyond the ideas of right-doing and wrong-doing there is a field. I'll meet you there." To understand this concept of God as all there is and also as all good requires us to transcend our earlier conditioning of judging life by its appearances. We must move instead to a higher state of consciousness where we believe with a deep faith in the unity of allness and goodness. Gradually our faith brings us to an understanding that all is good and good is all.

What are these people saying to us? They are telling us that the only reality of either good or bad is in the reality which we give to it by our own thinking, by our own feeling, by our own choices. This is not necessarily an easy concept to digest, for it implies a great deal of personal responsibility.

From time to time I hear someone go into great detail about what is wrong with their life. I won't list the specifics of what they say because it is all irrelevant to anyone other than them. They are not telling me anything about their physical situation. What they are telling me about is their choice of what they think and talk about. They choose to concentrate upon the limitations of negativity, upon problems rather than upon solutions. Therefore, their recommended solutions are often very dogmatic and demanding of others. They are under the mistaken impression that one can overcome challenges through sheer determined force alone.

We get caught in this trap of judging based upon appearances rather than judging based upon the truth because our physical senses require constant delineations and judgments in order for us to survive. We then take this discriminating thinking process and apply it to our entire lives. That's a mistake on our part, one for which we may never have been taught otherwise, but one for which we are individually responsible, just the same.

A similar mistake was made upon a social scale regarding work and jobs in the marketplace. This occurred as a result of the Industrial Revolution. The Industrial Revolution was merely a way of creating things or artifacts through a group effort which couldn't otherwise be created as efficiently and as expediently, and as cheaply, by individuals working on their own. This has worked well with physical production. But somewhere along the line someone observed that there was a conservation of work, and therefore dollars that might be applied to other areas of the workplace, places where the product was not something tangible, but rather something intangible. A product like information.

In other words, they decided to industrialize the office. And now we're all amazed that jobs are disappearing left and right, when that's part of the fallout of the industrial equation. We are presently in an incredibly huge transitional gap between an industrial society and an informational society in which we have yet to begin to adequately apply the equations of the informational revolution to our work situation. In a nutshell, "a job for everyone," was a creation of an industrial perspective that is quickly being replaced by an informational perspective. And that means that we're going to get to discover something else to do instead of being required to go to work for someone else.

This is what happens inside all of us. In our early development as human beings we create an efficient, expedient, cost-effective series of processes which are survival motivated and life enhancing within the parameters of our environment. Then, once we have those systems in place and our ongoing development exposes us to more complex issues of interaction upon more subtle levels of the invisible interactivities of metaphysical existence, we make the mistake of looking for the easy way out and we try to apply these already learned survival techniques to the more complex reality of thinking and feeling.

It's the difference between apples and oranges. And when you think about it and take a long, hard look at major institutional bodies, whether religious, political, or corporate, you can readily see that survival principles are at their core. But metaphysical existence is beyond survival. It is, instead, dealing with expansion, growth, and development because its existence is eternal. But if our attention is on merely surviving, then we can see that there is little time or opportunity available for expansion, growth, or development to express in our lives.

This all comes from the mistaken idea of judging good and evil. Now we've said that our belief is that God is all good. But we've also admitted that being good implies being bad. Here we have a fine line of semantics at a level of understanding that is beyond some people's present experience, for God is neither good nor bad. God merely is.

I've often said that I feel that the very best definition of God is, simply, that God is. Period. Nothing more to say. That says it all. God is. But our thinking processes won't allow us to let it go at that point. We're still caught up in the indigestion suffered from partaking of the fruit of the tree of the knowledge of good and evil.

Charles Fillmore tells us that trees "represent nerves," and that "nerves are expression of thoughts of unity; they connect thought centers." He says that the tree of the knowledge of good and evil "represents the discerning capacity of mind. Man first perceives Truth; then he must discern the relation of ideas before perfect activity is set up within him."

Why did God put that tree in the Garden of Eden? Was it as a temptation? No, it is placed in the garden because knowledge of good and evil, the choice of judging by appearances, is an option which is available to us. In fact, it's something which we can't completely escape on this plane of existence since we are constantly inundated with data gathered by our physical senses. Our brains are designed to take that gathered data, analyze it, categorize it, and file it. So, we're stuck, right?

No, God helps us. God says, "Don't eat it." That means don't digest it as though it were your source. You have but one source. That source is God. God is all there is. This out here is but appearance. If we allow it to become the source of our reality, then we have chosen to eat of the fruit of the tree of the knowledge of good and evil. And our lives become lives of constant judgment and we can never win, for being good implies being bad.

We must learn instead how to discover who we really are and then ways to allow more of that reality about ourselves to become more manifest in our lives and affairs.

So if it's okay for the tree to be in the garden then it must therefore be okay for the knowledge of good and evil to exist as options in our lives. Just don't consume it. Don't digest it. Don't make it a ruling part of your life. It's just a snack that enables us to more easily navigate the world of appearance.

And is not the goal of deep meditation, going into the silence, to transcend all judgment, both external and internal, all definition, and instead to "wait upon the Lord," to allow God to express itself to and through us? Then we have transcended the concepts of good and evil and have entered into the reality of God's very nature.

That God is all good is hard to believe as long as we contemplate it from a good verses a bad viewpoint. If, however, we can view it from a viewpoint of total acceptance, without judgment, then there is no other word for it but "good."

Many years ago I worked on an underground newspaper. I began as a writer and eventually I became the publisher. One of the earliest issues had a cover which said, "I am constantly awaiting the rebirth of wonder." That is the attitude, the approach, that we must assume as we contemplate God's all-encompassing is-ness, an attitude of wonder.

Think about a little baby and how its early life, before we have had the chance to interfere with its natural growing processes, is a life filled with wonderment. There is no judgment here, but rather an open acceptance, a joy and an expression of wonderment at the incredibleness of God's creation.

Jesus said that we must become as little children in order to enter the kingdom of heaven. He also told us that the kingdom of heaven is within us. So, in order to touch that kingdom that is within each and every one of us, that kingdom which is a realization of the total isness of God, we must approach it with a sense of wonderment, an openness, a trusting, believing faith in the overwhelming goodness of the allness. To argue with this belief that God is all good, is to choose to continue to feast off the tree of the knowledge of good and evil.

We must eventually come to the realization that there is another tree in the garden that we inhabit. It is the tree of life, and it is the field of all possibilities that is the truth of our being. God is all good because God is and God is all there is. Anything else, including the concepts of good or bad, are limitations upon that reality.

And that makes our belief systems different from many other Christians, for they are still caught up in the "us or them" games of separation created by the belief in good and evil. In reality, God is all good because good and evil don't exist. These are two different ways of looking at the concept of good. That God is all good has nothing to do with the good of good and evil. But for those who live in a consciousness of good and evil, there's no way to rationally explain why God is all good.

So God is all good, because semantically it's the best verbal communication description of the reality of God that we can come up with. Our claim of the goodness of God is in the realization that if God is all there is, then everything ultimately comes to the right end for everything is of God and always has been. When we look out at this vast universe in which we live, we realize that it has been functioning in a beautiful symphony of harmony for billions of years. Who is there who could call that infinite universe anything other than good?

Next we'll take on the big ogre. We're going to expose evil for what it really is. I'm going to tell you why evil doesn't exist, and then I am going to tell you why it does exist.

THERE IS NO EVIL

There is no evil; evil is actually a denial of the truth that there is no evil; evil's only existence rests in one's belief in its existence; therefore evil is the great lie of a belief in separation from God.

THERE IS NO EVIL

This is the big one. This time we take a look at that big bugaboo - EVIL. But first, just a little recap. We're examining what we believe that makes others look at us as though we were different. We began two chapters ago with the fact that God is all there is. Specifically, "God is all there is; absolute, total, without exception."

We followed that up in the last chapter with the realization that "God is all good, therefore everything that is, is good." Once we understand those two concepts, we are confronted with the question of what we're going to do about evil.

Our statement this time, therefore, is, **There is no evil; evil is actually a denial of the truth that there is no evil; evil's only existence rests in one's belief in its existence; therefore evil is the great lie of a belief in separation from God.**

This is a hard one to swallow for many who are bound up in orthodox conditioning.

I was talking with someone at a wedding once, and as is often the case, they wanted to know who and what I was: "are you a minister? What church are you from? Unity? No I don't really know what that is."

So once again I presented my brief 60-second introduction to Unity. To this he replied, "My wife and I grew up in the 'you name it' church, so we know what you mean by ritual because we're very grounded in it." See why I love talking with people?

Once at a **Whole Life Expo** in Atlanta, a man walked up to me and we started talking about Unity. When I mentioned that I grew up in Unity, he responded, "You're lucky. I grew up in the Whatever Name Church." And he walked away, his whole body literally shaking.

This is the conditioning of which I speak. And for those of you who came to Unity from a more orthodox background, you know just what I mean about ritual and conditioning.

The purpose of the teachings of Jesus was to help to free humanity from the bonds of appearances and to help us to regain our conscious connection with the truth of who and what we are. But his message didn't stop there. He then encouraged us to make that realization of the truth manifest in our lives and affairs. Those teachings of Jesus have, over the centuries, evolved into a movement which has become an institutional machine which has erected ritualistic monuments to Jesus the man, thus obscuring His message of the "Kingdom of Heaven Is Within You."

That is not so unusual. In Eric Butterworth's book, *Unity: A Quest For Truth,* he quotes a UCLA Professor who defined a concept which he terms "the 5 M's of Religion." Simply put, the professor claims that all religions go through five phases which he defines with 5 words, each beginning with the letter "M." He states that every religion begins with a single individual who has a unique spiritual experience which alters their life. Thus the first M is the **Man** or individual who has this initial, unique, spiritual experience. Because the experience changes this person's life, others are aware of the changes and either ask about its origins, or else the original person seeks to share the experience, and its results, with others.

This sharing process develops into the second M, the **Message**, a telling and a sharing and a teaching about this original spiritual experience.

As word spreads, the Message grows into the third M, which is the **Movement**. During this time, the Message begins to get altered through embellishment and the vagaries of retelling and translation.

Eventually the Movement becomes so large and scattered and the Message so altered from its original intent that efforts are made to control it so that it remains true to the original experience. These efforts result in the fourth M, the **Machine**. And with time the mechanics of the Machine become paramount in the so-called protection of the Movement of the Message of the Man who had the original experience.

Finally, the Machine, in an effort to justify itself, creates the fifth and final M, a **Monument**. Tragically, however, in every case, the Monument is always to the original Man or individual from whom this whole experience evolved, rather than to the experience itself, which first sparked the change in that individual and therefore sparks the promise of change for others.

Unity, I have always believed, floats between movement and machine with an occasional monument builder running around frantically trying to gather support for their latest creation. Furthermore, I have always believed that it is the ultimate purpose of Unity, and for all religious organizations, for that matter, to put themselves out of business. In other words, the purpose of all of this is to steer us back to the point where each of us has that original, spiritual, life changing experience. And when that is achieved, churches will no longer be necessary, for the guidance of all will come from within.

Now, for those of you who are attached to the idea of church, don't let what I've said worry you. I merely said that churches would no longer be necessary under this ideal scenario, not that they wouldn't exist. I'm sure that there will always be churches, though their activity and purpose will continue to change and evolve with time. This past evolution, or some might say devolution, of the church is, paradoxically enough, what has helped to make the Christian teaching last as long as it has. Tragically, that which has perpetuated the teaching has also adulterated it in its perpetuation.

This all ties in with our topic because the root of the belief in evil is closely aligned with the reasons that institutions get derailed from their original intent.

I'm sure we've all heard that evil is merely live spelled backwards: e v i l and l i v e . And there's a lot of truth to that, if you take life and what it truly is and then look at it backwards, evil comes into existence.

What do I mean by that? Well, what is life? Life is the expression of God as creator. We will be getting more deeply into this subject shortly, but for now realize that life is a constant unfolding series of infinite experience.

Have you ever seen a thunderhead cloud that was visibly in the process of growing? I mean that it was building so fast that you could easily see it move and expand. An incredibly powerful and beautiful experience; the cloud appears to expand from within itself in the same way that a balloon expands when we blow it up. Yet it has no visible outer shell holding it in. That's what life is like: it is expanding from the within to the without.

Vrle Minto, the founder of Alpha Truth Awareness Seminar, taught me that most people fail to realize that the universe has a natural flow to it. That flow is from being to doing to having. The entire universe naturally flows from being to doing to having. Now, if we stop for a minute and look at ourselves, and at those around us, we're likely to see a lot of people who appear to think that the universe flows from having to doing to being. We've all heard it: "If I only had it, then I could start doing the things that I want to and finally become who I want to be." Waiting around for a "have" so that they can finally "be." That's the hard way to do it. It can be done that way, but is it really worth it?

If, instead, we'll just be who we really are, then we'll begin doing what's in harmony with that being and the results will automatically manifest themselves. Now, if you'll think about that for a moment, you'll realize that is not something that we have to make happen in our lives through some sort of change. This is the way it already is. We merely need to alter our focus. So, the universe flows from being to doing to having. Being results in the action of doing which automatically manifests in having.

Yet, most people try to live their lives exactly opposite; they try to have so that they can do and then to finally become. And that's what evil is like; it is trying to live life backwards; it is judging life by its appearances, the results, the having, and then using that judgment to incorrectly work our way back to the source of the appearance. We must remember that the identity of all appearance is in our own choice of how we view the appearance.

Great spiritual belief systems have taught this truth for thousands of years; now science has joined in through the principles of quantum physics to give its stamp of approval to this expansive concept.

Our reality is not somewhere out there, friends, it is in here, within our very being, and we have the power to determine the kind of reality in which we live. And if we argue with that truth, then all we are doing is revealing to the world that we have chosen to be undisciplined, because to claim that the reality of appearance is more powerful than the reality that we are by our very nature is to say that the painting controls the painter. And though the essence of the painting facilitates a very powerful experience, the painter is still the creator. The painter can be the avenue for the painting's creation or the avenue of its destruction.

The painter is the channel, but a channel by choice, and it is that process of choice which is the key to the kind of world in which we live.

When we look at the book of Genesis for the story of creation, we have God creating Adam, the first man and then creating Eve, the first woman. Right?

Wrong! That's not what the Bible says. That's what the church says.

Here. Watch this. In Genesis One, verses 26 and 27, it says,

> *And God said, Let us make man in our image, after our likeness: and let them have dominion over the fish of the sea, and over the fowl of the air, and over the cattle, and over all the earth, and over every creeping thing that creepeth upon the earth.*
>
> *So God created man in his own image, in the image of God created he him; male and female created he them.*

It goes on in verses 28-31 to say:

> *And God blessed them, and God said unto them, Be fruitful and multiply, and replenish the earth, and subdue it: and have dominion over the fish of the sea, and over the fowl of the air, and over every living thing that moveth upon the earth.*
>
> *And God said, Behold, I have given you every herb bearing seed, which is upon the face of all the earth, and every tree, in the which is the fruit of a tree yielding seed; to you it shall be for meat.*

> *And to every beast of the earth, and to every fowl of the air, and to everything that creepeth upon the earth, wherein there is life, I have given every green herb for meat: and it was so.*
>
> *And God saw everything that he had made, and, behold, it was very good. And the evening and the morning were the sixth day.*

End of Chapter One. Note here that God has created man, in the plural "our" God's own image: male and female created he them. Some people read that and think that God created men and God created women. I believe that God created people and that he created every one of them male and female. And you may say, "That's a bunch of baloney!" And I say, "Go back and read it again, because that's precisely what it says. "And God said, Let us make man in our image, after our likeness. So God created man in his own image, in the image of God created he him; male and female created he them."

Sounds to me like God, "our image and our likeness" created plural man in God's image and likeness, both male and female. Not some male and some female but both male and female, in our image and after our likeness.

But that's just the beginning. None of this has to do with Adam and Eve. They have not been mentioned yet. End of creation; end of Chapter One. Mankind is upon the face of the earth and Adam and Eve have yet to show up. They are not the first in this story. They are "Johnny-come-lately."

Next we come to Chapter Two:

> *Thus the heavens and the earth were finished, and all the host of them.*

> And on the seventh day God ended his work which he had made; and he rested on the seventh day from all his work which he had made.
>
> And God blessed the seventh day, and sanctified it: because that in it he had rested from all his work which God created and made.
>
> These are the generations of the heavens and of the earth when they were created, in the day that the Lord God made the earth and the heavens,
>
> And every plant of the field before it was in the earth, and every herb of the field before it grew: for the Lord God had not caused it to rain upon the earth, and there was not a man to till the ground.

Now wait a minute. Didn't God create man in the first chapter, and now he's complaining because there is no man to till the ground. What's going on here? Well, first off, it's very obvious that Adam is not the first man. But apparently, for whatever reason, the men/women whom God had already created were not gardeners.

Finally, in Chapter Two, verse 6 God goes to work again. It must have been Monday. The sign of things to come. He works hard for six days creating the universe, takes a day off, and come Monday morning, he's got to go back to work again. Let's see what it says:

> But there went up a mist from the earth, and watered the whole face of the ground.
>
> And the Lord God formed man of the dust of the ground, and breathed into his nostrils the breath of life; and man became a living soul.

> *And the Lord God planted a garden eastward in Eden; and there he put the man whom he had formed.*

By now, you must have figured out that the man created in the first chapter is not the same as the man created in the second chapter. Why that is and what it means is not what we're looking at today. That's a story for another day.

Anyway, in the Genesis story of creation, we find Adam and Eve, Adam representing the first movement of mind in its contact with life and "substance," and Eve being feeling in individual consciousness, the feminine aspect of generic man. But Adam is told by God not to eat of the tree of the knowledge of good and evil before Eve even comes upon the scene.

Realize here, just as an aside, that in the order of the story in Genesis, God creates Adam, creates the garden, puts Adam to work, tells him to leave the tree alone, creates Eve, and then the serpent shows up and gets into a conversation with Eve about the tree.

Adam and Eve are symbols, aspects of generic humanity. They represent the developing movement of mind in its contact with life and substance, then developing from within itself feeling in individual consciousness. This then further evolves into our conversation with the subtlety of the temptation of our curiosity. Our curiosity is constantly enticed by the surroundings of appearances. Our feeling nature is fascinated by the world of appearance and it desires to give in to the temptation to consume it, to revel in it, with all of its pleasure and all of its pain.

Unlike the false belief of much of orthodox Christianity, Eve is not alone when tempted.

In Genesis Three: verse 6 it says:

> *So when the woman saw that the tree was good for food, and that it was pleasant to the eyes, and that the tree was delightful to look at, she took of the fruit thereof, and did eat, and she also gave to her husband with her; and he did eat.*

It says, "gave to her husband with her." It doesn't say that she took it home and fed it to him after he came home from his job of tending the garden. Adam was with Eve. Intellect and feeling were both a part of this temptation scenario

Feeling nature shared the knowledge of the concept of good and evil with thinking nature, because they are always together, different aspects of the generic being that they represent

Two verses later, it says:

> *And they heard the voice of the Lord God walking in the garden in the cool of the day; and Adam and his wife hid themselves from the presence of the Lord God among the trees of the garden.*
>
> *And the Lord God called to Adam, and said to him, "Where are you, Adam?"*
>
> *And he said, I heard thy voice in the garden, and when I saw that I was naked, I hid myself.*
>
> *And the Lord God said to him, "Who told you that you were naked? Have you eaten of the tree of which I commanded you that you should not eat?"*

What we're seeing here is that once we eat, partake, digest seeing things as good and evil, we become separate from God in our consciousness and this makes us feel naked and separate from God.

Who told you that you were naked? That's a lie that you have chosen to believe through the judging of good and evil. Because of our conditioning about evil, this is a pretty dramatic statement for many people to consider. After all, we all know that evil is rampant in the world. We only need to turn on the tube or pick up a paper to have confirmation of that fact. Yet how can evil exist if God is all there is and God is all good?

What is evil? Where does it come from? Why is it here? And just what do I mean when I say that there is no evil? Well, to answer those questions, I'm going to throw some more biblical scripture on you. Now, if you're not one who is into the Bible, don't let that disturb you. Just think of it as another ancient book with some interesting truths and mystical teachings. Take what works for you and don't worry about the rest.

In my growing up, the Bible was always there, but it didn't play the part of importance in my life that demanded the sacrifice that I saw in the lives of others around me. However, as I have grown older, I am drawn back time and again to the Bible as a reference tool because so many people have backgrounds in which the Bible plays a central position as a frame of reference for their lives. That's why I have continued to study with Dr. Rocco Errico and his work on the Bible. It helps to give me a way to relate to the perspective of others without having to get bogged down in the superficial mistranslations and misinterpretations which distort so many people's Biblical perspective, thereby keeping them in bondage to ideas that often have little connection to what the Bible really has to say.

It is a misinterpretation of the Bible, several hundred years after Jesus walked the earth, which today gives us the mistaken impression that we are sinners, worms of the dust, and that our bodies should be shunned and condemned. This erroneous belief is mistakenly attributed to the Garden of Eden story in the book of

Genesis. And it is further compounded in its distortions by a later claim that Jesus died "for our sins." In reality, a literal translation from original Aramaic text would say that Jesus died "because of our sins."

Jews don't believe or teach "original sin" as portrayed by the Christian Church in the story of Genesis. And remember, Genesis is a book of the Jews, of the Israelites. They don't see the story as the "fall of man." Again, that's a later Christian Church spin on an old Jewish story that, in turn, is a twist on even older, more ancient stories.

So, with that in mind, in an effort to understand the true nature of evil, I direct your attention to the book of John, Chapter Eight, verse 44. The setting is that Jesus is being questioned by the Pharisees. The Pharisees are a sect within Judaism which believed in absolute adherence to the letter of the law. It's interesting to note here that if you pull out a Thesaurus and look up the word "Pharisee" you will find that one of the synonyms is "hypocrite." Hypocrite is, of course, a word used often by Jesus, particularly in his confrontations with the attacks of the Pharisees. A hypocrite is one who puts on a false appearance of virtue and piety, who claims a belief in one thing but actually does another. Hypocrite is a word that always applies to those who insist upon demanding that others live by the letter of the law. This is impossible to achieve because the law is static while human beings are ecstatic.

When we say that the Pharisees were a sect of Judaism 2,000 years ago, it's good to remember that Jesus and his followers also became a Jewish sect while he was teaching. At the time it was probably thought of as the Jesus sect or the Nazarene sect. Only later, after Jesus' death, did the followers of the Jesus' teachings come to be known as Christians.

So the Pharisees are trying to verbally corner Jesus and reveal him to be a blasphemer. They believed in a God that had grown separate from His people, while Jesus taught a God accessible to all.

He emphasized this by teaching that the kingdom of heaven is within you. And so Jesus responds to the Pharisees by telling them that he is merely doing what the Father has directed him to do. This angers the Pharisees. They claim that their Father is Abraham, and they wish to know who Jesus means when he speaks of Father. Jesus then responds that Abraham is not their Father. He continues by saying:

John, Chapter Eight verse 44:

Ye are of your father the devil, and the lusts of your father ye will do: he was a murderer from the beginning, and abode not in the truth, because there is no truth in him. When he speaketh a lie, he speaketh of his own: for he is a liar, and the father of it.

That's the way the King James translation presents this scripture. A bit outdated with it's ye's and speaketh's. And what about that last phrase: "and the father of it."

Well, let's look at the same verse as translated by Dr. George Lamsa from Jesus' language, Aramaic, directly into English:

You are from the father of accusation, and you want to do the lusts of your father, he who is a murderer of men from the very beginning and who never stands by the truth, because there is no truth in him. When he speaks, he speaks his own lie, because he is a liar, and the father of lies.

"The father of accusation....A murderer of men from the very beginning ... who never stands by the truth, because there is no truth in him....He is a liar and the father of lies."

Now, "grok this," as Robert Heinlein's *Stranger In A Strange Land*, might say. Imagine for a minute that this "liar" is not a "being" at all, but is, rather, the "act" of lying itself. "A liar, and the father of lies." The lie itself.

When Adam and Eve "ate" of the fruit of the tree of the knowledge of good and evil, they were entering into a state of consciousness in which they were judging things by appearances rather than by the underlying truth of universal oneness. This physical world of appearance in which we are briefly expressing, "living" if you will, is a world of constant apparent opposites. It is therefore a continuous challenge to see beyond the appearance of good and evil and to recognize the underlying truth. What truth? Well, we're told that God made everything and that everything that God made was good. Anything in opposition to that would be a variance from the truth.

We're also told that humanity was created in the image and after the likeness of God. The world of appearances lures us away from remembering that truth about ourselves. And when that happens, we slip into the abyss where we begin to think and feel that we are separate and apart from God. Separate and apart? How ridiculous. We were created by God, from God stuff, and are expressing God in a creation of God. We cannot be separate and apart from God EXCEPT in our consciousness, in our beliefs.

If we choose to believe ourselves separate and apart from God, then we buy into the big lie. And from that lie, spring all of the other lies and deceptions. Just think about it. Think of any aspect of what we think of as evil and you'll see that underlying that expression of evil is a belief in separation from God. A belief in our oneness with God causes evil to disappear, for we cannot do evil when we recognize our oneness with God. We cannot even condemn evil when we are in tune with our oneness with God. And if you find that hard to swallow, then maybe, just maybe, you'll begin to understand why Jesus was seen as such a threat by the "leaders" of his time.

God created us in God's image. We created evil through judging by appearances rather than by the truth of our creation. Evil was created by our belief, and it is as strong as our belief, and it will continue as long as we believe in it and act accordingly. When we cease believing in evil by choosing, instead, to recognize our oneness with God, we act more Godlike and the former appearance of evil vanishes.

So, the bottom line is that there is no evil. However, evil will continue to be real and to exist for us as long as we believe in it and continue to deceive ourselves into believing that we are not one with God.

By the grace of God, there is no evil. By the creative imagination of man, evil appears to exist, and therefore, for all intents and purposes, it does exist, for those who believe it.

Next we'll examine just what God created when God created us.

WE ARE ONE WITH GOD

We are created in the image and after the likeness of God; the word for that creation is the Christ; it is the core of every one of us, without exception; we therefore cannot be separate from God for we are totally God in expression.

WE ARE ONE WITH GOD

Our next statement in *What We Believe That Makes Us Different* is: **We are created in the image and after the likeness of God; the word for that creation is the Christ; it is the core of every one of us, without exception; we therefore cannot be separate from God for we are totally God in expression.**

There is a lot of disagreement and misunderstanding throughout the Christian Church when it comes to just what God created when God created humankind. We have seen in scripture that in order, God created man, as male and female in his/our image and after his/our likeness. This is a God of infinite possibility - "our image and likeness" - and a God of oneness - "male and female." I believe that this verse tells us that we are each created male AND female, that we have both male and female aspects to our being and existence. The degree to which each of those expresses is dependent upon a number of factors, only one of which is physical gender. But there is more to who we are than physical gender, and with some people the usual expressions of physical gender are outweighed by other aspects of their sexuality.

I'll mention here something which may shock some people, and that is that we are sexual beings. The church has tried to deny that, glossing the facts over, and even condemning such an idea, and all of us sexual beings in the process. It's really rather crazy though, if, in Genesis Chapter One God created us sexual, male and female, that the church should then turn around and condemn God's creation. Of course, here we are on the edge of talking about sexuality other than the church approved heterosexuality, but we're going to save that for another day. Just suffice it to say for now that the Bible has very little of value to say on the subject of homosexuality. Those who refer to the Bible to bolster their homophobia are misunderstanding and misquoting the Bible and merely exposing their own ignorance, their meager distorted self image, and their lack of spiritual understanding.

For further examination of this subject I would invite the reader to check out my April 24, 2006 blog entry, "God, Man And Homosexuality," at "Still…..After All These Years" (http://zmajordomo.blogspot.com/) .

Anyway, God created us as sexual beings and our sexuality must be important for it is a very big drive for many people. I recall seeing this topic come up once because of an article in **USA Today** on Sex on the Internet. You may be interested to know that less than 5% of the websites on the Internet are sexually oriented. True, they draw a lot of "hits," as they call it when someone accesses one of them on the web, but they also draw a lot of hits from the media, who somehow seem to imply from time to time that it's alright for the media to give excess coverage and attention to the 5% but it may not be alright for the average citizen to give excess attention to these sites.

The **USA Today** issue, however, had an article which pointed out that all advances in media have been initially driven by strong sexual content. Some people may wonder why I would talk about sex in what might be considered a spiritual or otherwise religious book, but I wonder why people have problems with talking about the way God created us, whether it is in church or anywhere else. What are we ashamed of? Do we not know who we are? Most often, when people condemn others, what they are really doing is revealing what parts of themselves they fear the most. In other words they're saying, "I don't want you to do what I have a deep desire to do myself but am afraid of doing." I mention all of these things because until we come to terms with admitting who we are and accepting ourselves as who we are instead of judging and condemning ourselves, we're never going to be able to grow beyond that which we are judging, for that is where our attention is.

Some might say, "But admitting and accepting these things about ourselves will only lead to sin and anarchy." No, that is a false belief. I used to smoke. For the first 20 years of my life I was a passive smoker because my mother smoked. I was probably born with nicotine in my blood stream. Then, after trying very hard over a two year period when I became 20 I was able to finally become an active, addicted smoker, of cigarettes, pipes, cigars, and occasionally other substances. My tobacco consumption went on for 25 years at an average of two packs a day. That's over a third of a million cigarettes which I smoked during a quarter of this past century.

In 1990, I stopped doing that. I just made the decision that I was a non-smoker. I realize that I could become a smoker again, and very easily. All it would take is one cigarette and I would quite possibly be hooked again. So I just choose not to smoke, because it is no longer anything which I desire to do. I used to be a smoker. Now I am a non-smoker. And, you know what? Non-smokers don't smoke. So I don't smoke. Oh, it is an occasional temptation. And, actually, to be honest, every once in a while I will smoke a cigarette in a dream. But then again there are a lot of things that we do in dreams that we either wouldn't or couldn't do in "real life."

As I began writing this book, I opened the Bible Concordance that had been Mother's and I could smell the tobacco smell left over from the 50's, and the 60's, and the 70's, and the 80's. It is a smell that I am familiar with. It brings back many memories. But it is not a smell that I choose to recreate in my own life. It is, in fact, a smell that I find to be very offensive.

All aspects of our being are no different from my experience with tobacco. God gave us the ability to choose. We chose, through the Adam and Eve expression of our beings to eat of the tree of the knowledge of good and evil and therefore expand the scope of our choices. Ultimately we will choose to return to the Garden from which we banished ourselves and to no longer smoke the "experiences of manifestation." And until that time comes, we have plenty of time.

Each of us has our own row to hoe. Each of us has our own life to live. God created us unique. That is a subject which we will get into in a later chapter. But for now, be aware that we were created by God. All of this expression of a physical reality, and all that we are, is an expression of God. If it appears to be less than God, then that is because we are choosing to focus on that lesser aspect of its appearance, rather than upon the truth of its being.

Now, the word Christ does not appear in the Old Testament. So, from an Old Testament view, what is this Christ that Jesus became? Well, it is the image and likeness creation, the ideal spirit man. The we that we really are at the core of our being.

I draw your attention to Moses' experience with God on the mountain because this is a key to a great deal of our existence. You'll perhaps recall that "God appeared as a burning bush" and carried on a conversation with Moses. Finally, Moses asks who he should tell the Israelites has sent him on the mission that God has revealed to him. In the Lamsa translation, God self-identifies by saying "AHIAH ASHAR HIGH, THE LIVING GOD," to be known as "AHIAH." In the King James authorized translation, this has been interpreted to the phrase "I AM THAT I AM," with the shortened moniker of "I AM." This is God's name. It is our connection with the reality of who we are as image and likeness creations of God.

"I Am" is powerful magic. I discovered many years ago that it is possible to break out the sounds of I Am and to realize that it is comprised of every vowel, or open mouthed letter in the English alphabet and the letter M, which is the only consonant that can be pronounced with the mouth closed. This is an interesting vibrational mix.

There is one other word in the English language which contains these very same vibrational sound characteristics. That word is Om. I Am is a powerfully creative statement. How we use it, both verbally and mentally, determine the ways in which our lives and reality express themselves.

In classes that I have taught, and in churches I have ministered, I have stressed the importance of discovering how in tune we are with very positive aspects of our being. We can use the power of "I Am" to give us an instant awareness of just where we stand. This is a powerful technique that I learned from Vrle Minto. All we have to do is to take a word and say it followed by a resonating "I Am" and then listen to, feel, how our body, how our mind, how our feelings respond to that word coursing through our being on the vibrational sounds "I Am."

We can do this right now, this very moment. Let's try it together with the word Love. Let's try it aloud. We'll say "Love I Am." Together:

Love I Am.

Let the final sounds vibrate slowly to silence as one would do if chanting "Om." Do we resonate with that? Are we Love? Is there a part of us that says, "Oh, yeah?" Do we cringe? Or do we feel open, expansive, all-encompassing?

Now let's do Faith:

Faith I Am.

Can we resonate with the idea that we are positively expectant, open to all of the good that God has in store for us? Or, do we have the thought, "Who are you kidding?" pop into our head?

Now let's do Understanding:

Understanding I Am.

If being understanding of others is a problem for us, we might find a particular individual or group of people pop into your consciousness as the vibration of the "I Am" permeates our being.

Now, let's try the word, "Peace." It's important that we do this aloud so we can get the full effect of the "I Am" vibration, not merely an imagined effect.

Peace I Am.

Do we feel peaceful? Or do we feel agitated? If we're getting into the experience of this technique, we might wonder, and rightly so, if repeating any one of these statements more than one time might have the effect of altering our reaction. Try it and find out.

We'll try one more. The word, "Joy." This is an important aspect of our being that helps to keep us positive. Let's try it together.

Joy I Am.

If we find ourselves "glowing" then we want to remember to resurrect this feeling anytime we encounter anything that appears to be negative or in any way attempting to bring us down.

Dr. Timothy Leary used to say that if you take an upper person and a downer person and put them together in the same room, that eventually, in every case, the downer person will always bring the upper person down. The reason this happens is because downers suck energy. Therefore, I've always taught that the only way to deal with the downer people is to stay clear of them. Don't give them any energy to feed their downer experience. Although that may seem to be a hard thing to do, it is ultimately very kind. So if you encounter "downer" just raise your "Joy, I Am" vibration and be on your way.

When we listen to our responses to this exercise, realize that they may come in many different ways. Oftentimes when we pray, seeking answers, we refuse to see the answers that come to us. For instance, you might be praying for an answer on how to deal with a difficult person in your life. And instead of an answer you get a color, like orange or blue. Or you get the image of a tree or of a toaster. Or you get a word like "relevant" or "chew" or whatever. When this happens, people often wonder why God hasn't answered their prayers. Yet God answers all prayers. We ask the questions, the answers appear. They have no choice. That's the way the system works. In fact, if the truth be known, questions are merely the answers' way of making themselves known. The answers are already there. They already exist. They are merely looking for a way to manifest themselves.

Whatever your answer, whether a color, a word, an image, or a feeling, take that answer and call it forth in your awareness whenever you are dealing with the issue in question, the situation you were praying about. And then be ready to be amazed at miraculous works of the Father.

We are always one with God. We can't help but be since we are God in expression. Our purpose here is to consciously reestablish that God relationship in all aspects of our lives and affairs through our consciousness. Achieving that goal is easier if we understand the basics of communing with God, the divine operating aspects of what we like to call prayer.

Shortly before his passing, Charles Fillmore, co-founder of Unity, said that the greatest verse in the Bible was found in Paul's letter to the Colossians, Chapter One, verse 27. Now, remember, this is a letter that Paul is writing to a particular church regarding that church's issues. It is not written as global church doctrine. However, Paul has an interesting insight which he shares here. It is an insight which has far-reaching implications. I'd like to share with you verses 25 - 27:

> *For which I became a minister, according to the dispensation of God which has been given to me for you, fully to preach the word of God everywhere, even the mystery which has been hidden from ages and from generations, but now is revealed to his saints; to whom God wanted to make known the riches of the glory of this mystery among the Gentiles; which is Christ in you, the hope of our glory.*

That's right. This is the source of one of my 3 x 5 card "Remember" statements.

A fellow Unity minister once told me of a time when he was involved in a discussion about various scriptural passages with an extremely fundamentalist minister. Finally, when the conversation had escalated to the point of the fundamentalist's grilling of my friend over accepting the exclusive divinity of Jesus, my friend said, "But what about the scripture in John 14:12 where Jesus says, 'Truly, truly, I say to you, He who believes in me shall do the works which I do; and even greater than these things he shall do, because I am going to my Father.'" The fundamentalist minister replied, "Well, to tell you the truth, I wish that he hadn't said it."

Isn't that the way it often is when dealing with people who are so convinced that their opinion is right that they feel compelled to badger others into agreeing with them? They really don't want to hear about those ideas which are not in agreement with their own, even when it's reportedly the ideas of Jesus, himself. "I wish that he hadn't said it." There are a lot of things which Jesus said, and a lot of things which the Bible says, and a lot of things which many great religious and spiritual writings say, and a lot of things that just feel right, which many people would like to ignore.

From our original premise that God is all there is, it only follows that we, therefore, must be a part of that "all that is," and therefore a part of God. We then couch that in the terms that we are "created" by God.

Dr. Rocco Errico recently pointed out in a class that God never created anything. You can bet that that stirred up some brain corpuscles. The brain cells were popping like popcorn. Never created anything? Well, as Dr. Errico pointed out, the Second Law of Thermodynamics states that energy can neither be created nor be destroyed. So, if one thinks of creation as something appearing from nothing, that's just not realistic in the realms of physics. Therefore, rather than creating the universe, God transforms itself, that which already is, into universe.

Likewise, in "creating" human beings, God transformed itself into the existence which we call human. We are, therefore, God in transformation, God in expression, God in manifestation. We are in the image and after the likeness. And that creation that we are, in line with our second statement, "God is all good," must therefore mean that we are good. Humankind is the highest aspect of its idea-self that it can be. That's what you are, at your core. And the word for that highest manifestation of our selves, what Deepak Chopra calls the "field of all possibilities," is the Christ. That Christ is in you and is you.

However, the chances are that you don't know it. The chances are that you have very little awareness of who you truly are. The chances are that you devote the overwhelming majority of your time, your experience, your thoughts, your feelings, your life, to dwelling upon the appearances, to trying to figure out the right and the wrong of it all instead of just going on to Rumi's "field out beyond."

Think of it like this: Life is like a big wheel, the kind with spokes. Every one of us is a spoke on that wheel. Each one of those spokes is connected to the hub of the wheel. This is the commonality of our divinity which we all share. Whether we realize it or not, the hub is our source and also our destination.

At the opposite end of every spoke is the rim of the wheel. Each one of the spokes is connected to the rim in its own unique place. The rim is representative of the world of appearance. It looks different to each one of us. This visual example lets us realize that every spoke on the wheel is different and unique and yet they are all the same, for they are all spokes on the wheel of life. Each appears to be pointing in a different direction from all of the other spokes, yet they all share the same hub and a connection to the outer rim which circles upon itself infinitely.

One final observation on this image: when the wheel is in motion, rolling along, the closer one gets to the rim, the faster one is going. The closer to the world of appearance, the faster "things" appear to get. The closer to the hub, the smoother and easier the motion. It takes just as much time for the inner part of the spoke to make a complete circle as it takes the outer, rim-connected end of the spoke. The outer end just has to work harder and go further to get to the same location.

Jesus tried to tell his followers of the Christ within when he continually referred to God as Father. He would say, "My father," because it is a personal relationship, but he taught us to pray, "Our father," because that relationship is also personal for each and every one of us.

An early part of Christian Church history is the battle that took place between those who thought of Jesus as the "only begotten Son of God," and those who felt rather that Jesus was a wayshower who was setting the example for what each of us could recognize about ourselves: that each of us is the Christ. That battle rages on to this very day.

A cornerstone in this confrontation used by those who side with "only begotten" is, of course, John Chapter 3 verse 16: "For God so loved the world that he gave his only begotten son that whosoever believeth on him shall have eternal life." Of course, when looking at the original Aramaic, the word which has been translated all these years as "only begotten," could also be translated "like unto a firstborn."

The first born son in the Near Eastern family holds a high position of importance. It is through the firstborn son that the line of family heritage continues on, with all of the rights, and privileges, and possessions assigned thereto. "Only begotten of God" implies that God has stepped outside of God's own laws and principles to manifest itself. If God can create a universe containing over 70 septillion stars, isn't it incredibly humanly egocentric to think that God would need a woman's womb in order to replicate itself? Amazing that after thousands of years of the denigration of women by men that God would not be able to procreate without a woman's body to actually do the "work." Adam was created from dust, but for Jesus, God needed a woman's womb.

The church invented the story of Jesus' immaculate conception, implying that God was directly involved. But, because God is all there is, then God must be involved in every conception. Therefore, every conception must be immaculate. Anyway, either Jesus is "the" only-begotten of God or Jesus is to God "like unto a firstborn." And if "like unto," then why? Is it because he was some sort of trick baby or was it because he recognized his own divinity, the same divinity that lies within each of us, unrecognized? Which translation one chooses to believe depends upon one's own perspective, not upon any cut-in-stone truth.

In other words, what I am saying here is, if you choose to think of Jesus as God's only begotten son, that's okay. But you see it that way because that's the way you choose to see it, not because that's the "only" way that it is. When people have badgered me about Jesus being "God's only begotten son" I respond that I agree with them that

Jesus is God's Son, that he is God's creation, that he is God's outpicturing, God's manifestation, the Christ. But I also believe, and accept that they, too, are God's child, God's only beloved, the Christ.

Charles Fillmore says: "I AM is God's name in man; it is Jehovah, the indwelling Christ, the true spiritual man whom God made in His image and likeness. The outer, manifest man is the offspring of the I AM, or inner spiritual man. By use of I AM we link ourselves with outer seemings -- or we make conscious union with the Father, with Spirit, with abiding life, wisdom, love, peace, substance, strength, power, Truth, the kingdom of the heavens within us."

Begin reassuming control of your life by consciously directing your I Am in ways that reattach you to the Christ that is your true nature. You are the Christ. Rejoice in that awareness and go forth spreading joy and revolution.

One of the messages we can glean from the story of the Garden of Eden is that we have free choice. "And as Adam named it, so was it." The Adam part of us is constantly naming the various aspects of our reality. And as we name them, so they become "to us."

After considering all of the options and all of the arguments, we must each come back to the realization that the ultimate decision rests with us. How are we going to "name it?" Do we want to play the "worm of the dust" game? Or do we want to recognize the Christ indwelling each of us? Which perspective resonates with you? Which one feels right? My choice is the later. I behold the Christ in you and within all people, for the expression of God is infinite. Namasté.

GOD'S EXPRESSION IS INFINITE

What God does is to express itself; since God is all there is, then this expression is multitudinously infinite.

GOD'S EXPRESSION IS INFINITE

In the previous chapter we talked about Paul's revelation that your hope of glory is in the realization, and the release into expression, of the mystery that the Christ is indwelling YOU. Moving along in our flow of ideas, our next statement is: **What God does is to express itself; since God is all there is, then this expression is multitudinously infinite.**

It's difficult for many people to even begin to comprehend what this statement means. We are so used to judging by appearances that we're not going to give God credit for everything that appears to exist in the world. After all, if God were responsible for all of the stuff that's out there, if God were behind it all, then there'd be very little for us to hope for. After all, who would want to admit to themselves that they live in a universe designed and run by someone, or something, which would allow all of the negative which we see about us?

And yet, it all is God. And when we stop long enough to think about what the term, "all of it," really means, it can be somewhat overwhelming. All of it. All of the stuff that we can see, hear, taste, touch, and smell is God in expression. All that we can feel is God in expression. All that we can think and imagine is God expressing. Yes, thoughts, too, are expressions. That's why the Bible says even if you just think it in your heart it is the same as doing it.

And that's just scratching the surface, for it "always has been, is now, and always will be." Beyond the limitations of the concepts of time and space, God is expressing. Here's where I'm happy for the concepts of quantum physics and people like Deepak Chopra who help us to grasp the spiritual reality of the developing quantum scenario.

As I've already mentioned, Deepak reveals that quantum physics tells us that all possibilities exist. Fred Alan Wolf expands upon that and says that those possibilities exist as an infinite number of parallel universes. Deepak then adds that each of us, you and me and every single human being, is, at our core, a field of all possibilities. What that implies is that we are the connection between the possibility and its manifestation. And we'll be examining that awareness in greater detail in the next chapter.

But before we delve into the part we play in this infinite scenario, I want you to get a real feel for the unlimited infinity of God in expression. You may recall in the introduction I shared with you "In A Little Grain of Sand." That story helps to give us a greater perspective on the enormity of the infinity of which we speak when we make up terms like "multitudinously infinite."

You may recall that when they pointed the Hubble Space Telescope at an apparently empty spot in space, they discovered billion of stars. If you are a visually inspired person, the graphic results are on the internet at:

http://oposite.stsci.edu/pubinfo/pr/96/01.html

The bottom line is that the more we come to realize the overwhelming enormity of "God's kingdom," the less realistic the limitations of church doctrine become and the more meaningful the teachings of Jesus and other wise teachers becomes.

There is so much more to life than the mere limitations of our present physical expression and our myopic perceptions. God is all there is. God is all good. There is no evil, only gross misunderstandings of the truth, which results in creating evil results. But God's expression is infinite beyond even our wildest imaginations and the petty negative crap that we create and then dwell upon.

In 1976, Arthur C. Clarke, the author of *2001: A Space Odyssey* and the recipient of the original patent for the explanation of how to put satellites into geosynchronous orbit, published a book entitled, *Imperial Earth*. It is a sci-fi story about earth 300 years in the future, on the 500th anniversary of the signing of the Declaration of Independence.

As Dr. Clarke made the rounds promoting his book, he appeared on Tom Snyder's TV show, "Tomorrow," where Tom asked, "Well, tell us, Dr. Clarke, what will the earth be like in 300 years?"

Arthur replied, "Well, as you might imagine, I have a lot of friends who are scientists and also a lot of friends who are science fiction writers, and we discuss questions like that quite regularly. And the only thing that we can agree upon is that within 75 to 100 years we will have accomplished everything presently imaginable. Beyond that, our imaginations have yet to develop."

Friends, that was over 30 years ago. We now have only 45-70 years before we arrive at Dr. Clarke's prediction. We're rapidly speeding towards a future which is beyond the capabilities of our present imaginations. That's the infinity of God's creation waiting for us. That's the kingdom of God in expression. And I'll tell you something: I am excited.

In humanity's efforts over the years to understand the nature of God and the universe and existence, we have often chosen to couch our understanding within the limitations of appearances. What this does is to dramatically limit our options in life. If all of life is defined by appearance, then we cease to be open to that which has not yet appeared to our senses of appearance, specifically the senses of sight, sound, taste, touch, and smell. One of the great dangers in doing this is that we extremely limit our options. What's more, we end up placing an undue emphasis of our focus upon that small aspect of reality which is appearing at the present time in our sense of reality.

For many years now, I have referred to the Firesign Theater, a comedy group of yesteryear, and their 1972 record album, entitled

"Everything You Know Is Wrong." One of the reasons that I believe the statement of that title is true is because most people are totally caught up in the appearances without understanding or giving due credit to the source of the appearances. They therefore may see the picture without really knowing what the picture is of. And that's what we're talking about here. The source. And once we consider the source, then we want to understand how it expresses and what therefore our priorities of importance are.

God is all there is. When something happens like Princess Diana's fatal crash, or the fatal crash of John Kennedy, Jr.'s plane, or the tragedy at Columbine High School, or the explosion of the Space Shuttle Challenger, or the tragedy of September 11, or the senselessness of what happened in any number of other shocking interruptions to life as we believe we know it, our sources of information, the media, concentrate upon the morbidity of what happened. And when I say concentrate, we all know that it's really super concentrated. And nowadays in the new theology of the media, what they are doing is looking to see where they can place blame and whom they can shame.

Marshall McLuhan, the major media guru of the previous century, pointed this out to us decades ago. He told us that it is the nature of the news to be negative. Understand what I'm saying here. It is the nature of the news media to focus upon the negative aspects of life. What do I mean by negative? I mean those aspects of life that we wish hadn't happened. We seem to be fantastically intrigued with, and drawn to, that which we can feel sorry about with a morbid fascination. Why is this? Well, let me tell you two true stories to illustrate how this has happened, and then we will examine what we can do to correct it by refocusing our attention upon the truth of our fifth statement and the options which it presents for us.

In the 70's when I worked for General Motors, the division where I worked, Delco Products, made all the shock absorbers for all

GM cars and trucks in the world and for a number of vehicles made by other manufacturers. While I worked there, Delco cut a deal with Opel to make shocks for them. There was one hitch, however. Since Opel was a German company, Delco was bound by the same legal standards which applied to Opel. These were German government standards, and what they required was for Delco to manufacture a shock absorber that would last the life of the car, rather than the shocks they were making for Americans that needed periodically to be replaced.

"No, problem," they said. "We've always been able to do that. But it will cost you more." "We know that," said the Germans. "But safety is worth the extra price to us. That's why we have instituted these laws to require quality product." Well, Delco was in a quandary. Should they continue to make inferior shocks for their American cars and build new production lines to make superior shocks for the Germans, or should they just go ahead and upgrade all of their production lines to make superior shocks for everyone and just pass the cost along to the American consumer. Of course, they upgraded across the board and passed the cost along. But the question arose as to why they hadn't provided the better product years ago. GM's answer was that the Americans weren't willing to pay for quality and safety.

Well, historically, that's a bunch of crap. General Motors is a company made up of hundreds of small auto companies which were bought out and merged into the GM monolith back before most of us were born. The one major competitor whom they weren't able to buy out was Ford. And ol' Henry Ford was a pain for them, because he kept trying to make better vehicles while GM's emphasis was upon appearance rather than content. That means that each year the styles changed, but the operational changes were slow in coming. So, although GM's claim is that Americans didn't want to pay for safety, the fact is that GM chose appearance over content and then sold that concept through their advertising in order to increase their profits. In other words, the people had come to expect what they were conditioned to expect as a result of the conditioning of advertising.

Advertising and its impact. In 1990, as I have told you, I stopped smoking. I had smoked over a third of a million cigarettes during the preceding 20 years. A friend of mine had quit smoking several months before I quit and her ability to do so had inspired me to believe that I could do the same. The way she quit was interesting. She said that if your best friend dies, no matter how you feel about it, or what you do, you cannot change the fact that they are dead. You cannot bring them back. They are dead. They are gone from this level of existence, and that's that. You can remember them, but they can never be there with you the way they were when they were alive. So, she determined that cigarettes had become her best friend. Then she chose to let her best friend die. Once dead, there was no turning back, no matter how much she missed them. She quit smoking, just like that. It was a choice. It was a decision.

Well, what made this episode of particular note was that some time later I got a copy of Science News, a weekly that shares the latest in scientifically reported discoveries. The cover story was upon the effects of advertising in the selling of cigarettes. The cover contained an ad from the 1930's showing a very stylishly dressed woman smoking a cigarette. In the smoke coming from the end of the cigarette it said, "I am your very best friend." An idea planted 15 to 20 years before my friend was even born.

These slogans hang around. I'll give you an example. Here's a popular slogan. I'll give you the first part and you supply the last word. Okay? "Pepsi Cola hits the ...." Do you know the last word in that jingle? It may be of interest to you to know that that slogan has not been used in advertising since 1959. Fifty years. And yet it's still remembered by many to this day. Oh, the end of the slogan, of course, is that it hits the "spot." I sometimes drive our kids nuts because I teach our grandkids how to sing decades-old advertising jingles.

The point here has to do with the focus of our attention. If God is all there is, then why do people so often focus upon the limitations instead of upon the possibilities. The answer is that we are encouraged, conditioned, cajoled, enticed, entrapped into doing so. God gave us the ability to choose and the media of communications which we have created have narrowed our focus of attention to be upon limitation rather than upon possibility. Even our entire economic system is focused upon keeping people just at the edge of getting by. But that's not what life is truly all about.

Contrary to the teachings of Jesus, most religions on this planet, including major portions of Christianity, preach lack and misery as the reality, as what life on this physical plane is all about. I once met with an Islamic group to tell them about Unity, and several people there informed me that this life is a life of misery and that good only comes after judgment for those who go to heaven. If that's true, then I want to know how you can explain this. Three hundred fifty years ago, there were about 550 million people on this planet. That's about twice as many people as there are in the U.S. today. A hundred years later, when the U.S. was founded, the world's population had grown by almost 200 million (or by about a third) to 725 million people. One hundred years later, in 1850, there were 1 billion 175 million people on the planet. In the next 50 years, by 1900, that total jumped by 424 million people to a whopping 1 billion 600 million. That was a little over 100 years ago. Just a little over 1 ½ billion people; a threefold increase in just 250 years.

At that time, one hundred years ago, only 5% of those people had adequate food, clothing, and shelter. That 5% totaled about a meager 80 million people. Not all of them were in the United States, though most of them probably were. That's very close to the number of people that presently reside in the four largest cities on the planet: Tokyo, Mexico City, Mumbai, and São Paulo. Five percent, or 80 million people with adequate food, clothing, and shelter; the other billion, five hundred twenty million people going without; just 100 years ago. But by 1970, for the first time in history, half of the world's population had adequate food, clothing and shelter. At that time, just over 30 years ago, the world population was about 3 3/4 billion people, which means that the "haves" totaled about 1 billion, 900 million people. Or more people than there were on the entire planet just 70 years earlier. That's a 2300% increase in just 70 years of those moving up to joining the ranks of the "haves."

In the past 30 years the world's population has almost doubled, which means that the number of halves has probably at least doubled also. And how many people are there now? Well, we have passed the 6 billion mark and there seems to be no real signs of slowing down. That means that over 3 billion people are now haves, with adequate food, clothing and shelter. And that's only if the overall percentage has remained at a constant 50% after a 2300% growth rate over the preceding 70 years. In the last one hundred years, the number of haves in the world has grown from 80 million to over 3 billion, or a 3,800% increase, while the number of have nots has grown from one billion, 520 million to somewhere under 3 billion, a doubling or less than 200%. This, while the world's total population has grown by 375%.

So, in spite of claims of lack and misery as the reality of existence in the world, we see that there is an exponential improvement over the years in the lives of people. Much of our lives, and certainly of our economy, is founded in a belief in the inevitability of scarcity, which is in direct contradiction to the reality of the viral spread of success.

In opposition to the religious teachings of "life equals lack," I believe in the infinite abundance of God, of the universe. And it is obvious that life, itself, is a major channel through which that abundance becomes manifest. The higher, or more evolved the consciousness indwelling life becomes, the more complex and beautiful are the potentials of its manifestation.

Around 1950 or so, Arthur C. Clarke wrote a story in which he claimed that every person on the planet stands in front of 30 ghosts. What he meant is that if you take the world's population and multiply it by 30, you'd have the total number of human beings who have lived on this planet since humans took their first step. Well, in 1950 there were about 2 ½ billion people, so 30 times that means that there have been roughly 75 billion people who were born, lived and died on this planet since the first human appeared. Because there are so many more people alive now, compared to 50 years ago, we each now stand in front of only 13 ghosts instead of 30 ghosts of 1955. Well, after all, there are just so many ghosts to go around.

What was all of those people's purpose in life? Probably, many of them lived in order to try to provide a better world for their children and for their children's children. They wanted their offspring to have it better than they did. Well folks, if you look around you, you'll see that it's finally happening. After millions of years on this third stone from the sun, humanity has evolved to a place where it is now the channel for incredible wealth. And yet, there are people who claim that one of the major problems with people today is their desire for instant gratification. Instant gratification? Seventy five billion human beings suffered and gave their lives to create what we have today. How can one call accepting what's taken millions of years for humanity to manifest mere "instant gratification?"

Jesus said, "Consider the lilies of the field: they toil not, neither do they sow, yet not even Solomon in all his glory was arraigned as one of these." Friends, we live in a reality, in a time, when the abundance of God is expressing in more ways than we can even begin to comprehend. Yet we've got people running around telling us to ignore this divine manifestation and to instead practice deprivation and suffering. That's not what I grew up learning in Unity. Unity taught me that I am God's child and as such I am an heir to all good. Not someday, but now. AND, Unity taught me that that same truth applies for everybody, right here, and right now.

And how does that good come? In the Gospel of Matthew we read: "Seek ye first his kingdom and his righteousness (or its right useness) and all these things shall be added unto you." The Jews looked for a savior, a redeemer, a Messiah for so long that they didn't even recognize one when he arrived. In a like manner, people have desired the wealth that is their divine birthright for so long that they don't even recognize it when it finally manifests.

And it all boils down to a matter of perspective. I recently talked with a young man who said, "I'm tired of hearing people tell me how much harder it was in their day. In the fifties, you could raise a family of five working in a drugstore," he said. Is it harder now, or was it harder then? It all depends upon how we choose to look at it.

What God does is to express itself. Now the reason I say "itself" instead of "himself" is because God is not a him. God is not a man. God is spirit. Genesis talks about God's creation of humankind, first saying that God created humankind in our/his image and after our/his likeness, male and female created he them. Male **and** female is therefore the image and likeness of God.

In our language we don't have a pronoun to adequately express this sexual completeness, so I feel that the most feasible course is to opt for the word "it." There were times in my past when I tried to use newly coined pronouns. You know, things like "herm" and "hisr," or something like that. But I've come to like "it" because it keeps us away from the temptation to concentrate upon the differences of sexual expression and instead it focuses upon what I think of as the all-encompassing generic possibilities.

So, the work of God is to express itself. We could call it God's job, except a job requires a boss, and God doesn't have a boss. God is what one would call self motivated. That's an important awareness in and of itself. If God has no boss and God is self motivated and God created us in that likeness and image, then doesn't that imply that neither do we have to have a boss and aren't we therefore self motivated? Of course that leads us back to a realization that keeps popping up in my teaching, and that is that we are therefore the ones who are responsible for the outcomes, for the happenings of our lives.

Some people might say that we're limited by the circumstances of our lives in what we can do. But I choose to believe that the possibilities are endless. An example of that is actually a deep part of our belief system. That's why many folks believe that Elvis is still alive. Friends, the possibilities which are open to us are limited only by our own belief in limitations. God expresses itself and since God is all that there is, that expression, therefore, is multitudinously infinite.

We have an interesting trinity developing here: ancient truths from many spiritual disciplines, quantum physics, and the teachings of Christianity, all revealing the same truths from different perspectives. Remember that we are a field of all possibilities, and that all possibilities exist. So let's look, once again, at how God does what it does, how it expresses itself, and what that means to us as creations of, as children of, God, and how it therefore affects the affairs and aspects of our reality.

First we must understand that the true, full nature of God is beyond our ability to comprehend. Ever. It is a mystery which we can pursue but which will never be totally revealed to us. That is the way it must be for God to be all there is and to be, therefore infinite. If we could comprehend the allness of God then God would be finite, limited. And God would not be one, but would be two. But God is not limited. God is unlimited.

Perhaps we can get a general grasp of the reality of this divine expression by looking at it like this. God is all there is. But all what? All possibility. And in order to be what it is, it must therefore express. As it expresses, the thought occurs that it can either express chaotically, or it can express in an orderly fashion. For many years, science has generally proposed that the universe began as what they call "the big bang." I believe you'll find, according to the big bang theory, that this expression begins omni-directionally in a very chaotic and explosive manner some 13 ½ billion years ago. But it very quickly begins to order itself.

This self-order comes initially in the form of principles, principles which have to do with very elementary, basic expressions of being, such as energy and force. Light is an expression of energy. Gravity is an expression of force. Both light and gravity function, or operate, according to a standard set of principles. These principles are what we may think of as the laws of God. They self-actualized, came into initial expression, because they were the most efficient way for the expression of God to manifest itself. God expresses with order, efficiency and balance.

Those basic, self-appearing laws of God's expression then become the foundation, the basis, for that expression to manifest itself in an infinite number of ways. When we say manifest, from an actual scientific understanding of what is happening, we realize that through the interplay between various expressions of energy and force, and based entirely upon principle, patterns of interference come into existence. This is a positive interference. It is a creative interference. It is a complex interference. It is a growing interference which results in patterns which not only are the basis of everything that we sense but they even totally comprise our ability to sense these aspects of patterned reality.

Remember, quantum physics tells us that not only are all possibilities possible, but that all possibilities exist. In other words, God is not linear, but God is instead infinitely omni-directional. Let me see if I can add some clarity to that realization. If God is all there is, and that all there is is in a state of total expression, then it is ludicrous to think that its expression would, in any way, be limited. So, the principles which have self-actualized in the ongoing expression of God are not God themselves. They are only the most efficient framework within which God expresses. And that framework is limitless.

One of the results of the interactions of these principles is the existence of consciousness. Another is the existence of the concept of space. Still another result is the concept of time. But, we're now coming to know and realize and understand that time and space and consciousness are far greater in their expression than our meager understanding of them to this point in our existence.

Space and time are relative. What does that mean? It means that their meaning to us is dependent upon our perspective. And what is our perspective? It is the view which we choose to focus upon. Time and space, are, therefore what we choose them to be. For most people, their view is very narrow. But it need not be. Now, to expand our view is not easy. Why? Because all around us there are people, other aspects of consciousness, who still hold on to narrow, limiting views. But just because it's difficult to shift our perspective doesn't mean that it is impossible.

For every one of us, learning to drive a car was not easy, yet it wasn't really that hard. Why wasn't it that hard? Because we were familiar with automobiles before we ever drove one. They have been a part of our lives for as long as we have been alive. But imagine for a moment what it must have been like for people who were born before the advent of cars to suddenly see one for the first time and to get in right then and there, on the spot, and learn how to drive it. We've all seen movies in which people, from decades before, can't seem to control an old car, even though it's only going at a blinding speed of 5 or 10 miles per hour. You know, there was a time when it was believed that we'd never be able to go faster than 50 miles per hour. Yeah! It was predicted that the human body could not stand the pressure of speed above 50 miles per hour. And one of the early people at Rolls

Royce predicted that there would never be more than 5,000 cars in the entire world ... because, after all, there weren't any more chauffeurs than that. People, it's all a matter of perspective, a matter of how we choose to view what we call reality.

Well, changing our perspective is not as hard as learning to handle something that is totally alien to us. That's because changing our perspective is something which we do all of the time. We have to in order to survive.

Several years ago, late at night, the world changed dramatically. One day we lived in a world which contained a Princess Diana. The next day we lived in a world where there was no Princess Diana. Like it or not, a part of our perspective of reality changed. She was here to be hounded and photographed and to have her image sold from millions of newspaper racks, and then she became instantly resigned to history. There will be no more pictures. She will never be any older than 36. The same thing holds true for John and Carolyn Kennedy Jr. and Lauren Bessette. The same can be said for others with a world impact: John Kennedy, Robert Kennedy, Martin Luther King, Jr. But, in fact, the same thing holds true for all of us, though most of us enter that transition from this level of existence to the next one with some form of notice that it is coming rather than having it unexpectedly squeeze the very breath out of us.

Life is full of constant change. Some changes are big and some are small. Yet life, itself, goes on. Now, if God expresses in an infinite multitude of ways, then we may be able to choose which of those expressions is the reality in which we reside. And, in fact, that is already the truth of our existence. We have the power to choose the reality in which we live. It would therefore be to our benefit to choose a reality which is in line with our purpose and with our desires. And what is our purpose and what are our true desires? Well, isn't that what we're each trying to discover? And once found, we're seeking ways to achieve that purpose and to see those desires manifest in our lives. And that's what all of this is about. Helping us to discern who and what we are and what we can do about it.

Next we'll take a deeper look at our incredible uniqueness and its relationship to the Christ and the infinite expression of God.

YOU ARE UNIQUE

As an expression of God, each of us is unique, a singularity; Jesus is a unique expression of God; you are a unique expression of God; everyone and everything is a unique expression of God; no one individual expression is better or worse than any other expression; each is a singularity; each is absolutely, totally, uniquely, singularly, exquisitely, fully God in expression.

YOU ARE UNIQUE

We have talked about the infinity of God's creation. And I steered you to some incredible photographs taken by the Hubble Space Telescope that should give you a broader appreciation of the vastness of this infinite creation in which we presently live. I talked with someone recently who proposed that the whole universe is falling. To do that would imply an up and a down. What we're talking about is beyond the limitations of appearance. The universe is not falling; it is being. The idea of its "falling" is a rather outdated and primitive concept.

Two chapters ago, we talked about the realization that the Christ Spirit, that perfect idea human being Genesis creation of God, resides within each and every one of us. Now, I want to talk about what happens when we couple our inner divinity with the infinity of creation.

Our sixth statement is: **As an expression of God, each of us is unique, a singularity; Jesus is a unique expression of God; you are a unique expression of God; everyone and everything is a unique expression of God; no one individual expression is better or worse than any other expression; each is a singularity; each is absolutely, totally, uniquely, singularly, exquisitely, fully God in expression.**

The infinity of God allows for an infinity of expressions. I like the term "singularity." It implies a uniqueness which is, nevertheless, a complete oneness and wholeness. It is such a beautiful paradox of life that each of us is, at our core, that single perfect creation of God, and yet each of us is absolutely, totally unique.

Recently, scientists working in the genetics of cloning have learned that although they can create seemingly identical physical living beings, that those beings develop their own uniqueness within their identicalness. So, although they start out from a physically identical blueprint, their development takes them in individually unique directions. Life is infinite, in spite of our attempts to compartmentalize and pigeon-hole it.

Recall in our previous chapter that Dr. Arthur C. Clarke said in 1955 that behind each and every human being stand 30 ghosts. And based upon his claim I estimated the total number of human beings who have inhabited this planet at about 75 billion people. Seventy five billion people over the course of this planet's long history and no two alike. Each one individual. Each one unique. Each one different. Each one special. Each one a singularity.

Our purpose with this statement is to enter into a fuller realization of our own individual uniqueness and through that awareness to come to understand how important each of us is. Important? Of course. God created you in God's image and after God's likeness. God breathed the breath of life into your nostrils. Think about that for a moment. Right now you are breathing. Be aware of your breathing. The air is pulled in. The air is expelled. In, out, in, out. Even when we're asleep or otherwise unconsciousness. In, out, in, out. How does it do that? Constantly. In, out, in, out, in, out.

Without that breath, you will cease to exist on this physical plane. And your ceasing to exist will be rather quick, in a matter of minutes. And before you know it, the you, as you have been identified since leaving the womb, will join the long line of billions who have gone before. The you that you are has never been before now and it will never, ever be again. Some might find that realization sad. But sad is merely a choice. One can also choose to feel privileged and blessed. And remember that beyond this experience on the physical plane of existence lies an infinite number of possibilities of new experiences of uniqueness.

Our uniqueness is a blessing. But it is a blessing which few recognize during their brief existence as the unique singularity. Instead we are seduced by the world of appearances into believing that we're all supposed to strive to be alike. Same food, same clothes, same houses, same schools, same jobs, same vacations, same likes and dislikes. And yet, the true singularity within is continuously struggling to make its presence known. I am unique. I am special. You are unique. You are special.

Now, here's where I sometimes get into trouble with my more conservative friends. It goes something like this:

THEM: "Do you believe in the divinity of Jesus Christ?"

ME: "You bet I do. I believe that Jesus was created in God's image and likeness."

I pause here while that sinks in. Then, before another word is spoken, I add,

ME: "But I also believe in **your** divinity. In fact, I believe in the divinity of every human being. I believe that God created all of us and that God has a personal relationship with each and every one of us like that of a parent and a child. That creation that we are is often called the Christ, and when Paul said, 'the mystery hidden for ages, but now revealed….is Christ in you, the hope of glory,' I take him at his word."

As Deepak Chopra says, at our core we are each a field of all possibilities. I concur totally. I go on to state that anyone who denies or belittles this view is endeavoring to destroy the self-realization of divinity within others and should therefore be avoided. It is not the nature of God to tear down but rather to build up. For all the apparent destruction throughout the universe, the fact is, by evidence of observation, the universal creation of God has grown to a degree and a magnitude that is pretty much beyond our comprehension. I want to make certain that I am perfectly clear here. God builds far more than

God appears to destroy. And the apparent destruction, when viewed on a grander scale, seems always to lead to new and more elaborate creations.

This was the underlying thrust of Jesus' teaching. His was a teaching of inclusion rather than exclusion. Those who promote exclusion in the name of Christian teachings are not truly Christians, for they are not following the example set by Jesus but instead are using pieces of church doctrine to promote their own agenda. They would better be called Churchians. In the kingdom of God which Jesus proclaimed, there is room enough for everyone. And that only makes sense when one recognizes the inherent divinity of every single human being.

It's funny, but sometimes when I am composing text like this, I can hear, in the back of my mind, various people whom I have known who, in response to what I am writing, in my imagination, start spouting scripture at me to contradict what I am writing.

Decades ago I realized that the scriptures cannot be the "absolute revealed word of God," as some would propose, because there were so many contradictory scriptures within scripture. But just because there are inconsistencies in the scriptures doesn't mean that they must be totally discarded. To do so is just as senseless as declaring that they are the revealed word of God. People who embrace either of those extremes know little about scripture and even less about the history of the scriptures.

In spite of the literal inconsistencies there is ample evidence that there are a number of profound truths contained in the Bible. And our knowledge of these truths can contribute to our living happier, more fulfilling lives. And the desire to seek and to share in this awareness of who and what and why we are is behind my motivation for writing this book.

Anyway, a large part of the thrust of Jesus' ministry and teachings was in describing, through direct teaching and through parables, the truth about our being, that we are children of God. And that truth expresses in a multitude of ways, each of which is a unique singularity.

This life that you are presently living, is a once in a lifetime opportunity, a once in eternity opportunity. You are unique and this is a unique opportunity. What are you going to do with it? The same thing as always? The same thing as others? If either of your answers is yes, then you might occasionally want to ask yourself the question, "Why?" If God created you to be unique, why try so hard to be something that you are not?

The context of this chapter's statement was the origin of the original title for these ten statements that we're studying. I had initially called it *Apprehending and Comprehending the Singularity,* because the uniqueness of our being is an important focal point of our search for the truth. Recognizing our singularity, our uniqueness, requires that we detach from our attachment to all appearances, for any kind of connection with appearance negates the uniqueness of our singularity.

The reason that we are unique is because there is no reason for God to express redundantly. Previously we explored the fact that God's expression is multitudinously infinite. This infinite expression negates the necessity for duplication. This is a very important realization about the truth of all creation. If there is no duplicity, then there is an equality of importance to all of creation. This is an idea which underlies major spiritual disciplines all over the world. This, by its very nature, opens the door to our being, to the realization that there is a special sanctity to all of life. What's more, that sanctity extends to all of creation.

Now, this belief can lead to an impractical overreaction to the importance of the uniqueness of all existence. We've all heard about the sacredness of Brahman cattle in India, or monkeys in Cambodia, or we've heard about people who are careful not to even harm a bug.

When I was on Midway Island during my time in the Navy, we shared the island eight months out of the year with Albatrosses, otherwise known as Gooney Birds. We were under orders based upon national law that we were not to touch or otherwise injure any of those birds, no matter how much they might bug us or otherwise interfere with our duties.

All cultures and belief systems have various aspects of creation which they consider with a sense of importance which exceeds the rest of creation. We even do this in our personal lives with our feelings for those we love or those who are close to us particularly through blood connection.

This brings us to an interesting distinction in our awareness which affects our entire lives as far as how successfully we are able to be willing, open, knowledgeable channels for the expression of God. Let's see if we can make this conundrum clear in a way that will make it easier for us to be more in tune with this divine expression which is our purpose for being.

We begin with the fact that God, the source of all that there is, expresses in an infinite number of ways. Every aspect of existence is unique. Everything is, therefore, special, for there is none other like it in the entire universe of manifestation. Yet, because everything is totally an expression of God, therefore everything is equal, for it is absolutely, totally God in expression. Everything is what it is, nothing more and nothing less, but totally God. Therefore nothing is anymore special that anything else. No one is more important or special than anyone else.

This can appear to be a contradiction. Everything is special, yet nothing is special. Each of us is special, yet none of us is special. That is the nature of reality. It is a paradox, a seeming contradiction.

Why does this contradiction exist? Well, we need to understand that the contradiction is not in the creation itself. The contradiction is in our perception. It is possible for these seemingly opposite aspects of expression to exist simultaneously, in apparent opposition to one another without actually being in opposition.

Let me give you an example. Let's consider the question, "What is life?"

Science has tried to identify the answer to this question by trying to quantify physical differences in people when they die. The latest I've heard is that they might have found a slight difference in a body's weight at the moment of what we call death, yet it is so minute that it's almost negligible. And they still don't know what it is that they might be weighing when the change of death occurs.

I grew up with the belief that life is eternal. Why is that? Well, for one reason, because there is no evidence to prove otherwise. There are, throughout history, reported experiences implying that life continues to exist beyond the death of the physical body, and that it can even be communicated with. A basic tenet of Christianity is a belief in the eternality of life, as epitomized by the resurrection and ascension of Jesus. The Christian religion, the Christian belief, includes a belief in, and acceptance of, the eternality of life.

So here we have what we know and believe to be an experience which we know as life eternal. And yet we also have death. And often those who profess the loudest to be believers in the one also most adamantly fear the other. It's like the old song that says, "Everybody wants to go to heaven, but nobody wants to die." This is truly a contradiction in belief, and yet there is plenty of room for such contradiction in our consciousness.

Shortly before my Father, LeRoy DeTurk, died, I wrote to him asking questions about his life before I was born. That was a subject that I knew very little about, for he had been married previously to his marriage with my Mother and he didn't desire to share much with me about that previous experience. In fact, following my father's passing, I learned that my oldest half brother was shocked to discover that my father had absolutely no photographs of my half brother's mother, my father's first wife. But in shutting off that portion of his life, it left a gap between what I knew about him from experience and what I knew of him from hearsay.

In my letter I told him that I had come to realize that I knew and believed two different stories about his early life which were in direct contradiction with one another and yet I firmly believed them both, even though it was not possible for both of them to be true. Yet for me, they were both true.

In one story, he left home at the age of 14 and was on his own thereafter and taught himself piano and became a freelance entertainer. Yet, in the other story he lived with an aunt and an uncle and went to school at Ohio State University, where he was in the Glee Club, and he also attended Northwestern University. Obviously the second story was the true one, for I had seen photographs of my Father in the glee club. Yet that never detracted from my belief in the other story. That is until he responded to my letter and set the record straight. I had been able to believe in both stories for years because I never thought about them both at the same time until I wrote him that final letter.

Our lives are filled with just such contradictions, such paradoxes of belief. The fact that everything and everyone is special and unique, and at the same time everything is equal is just such a paradox.

Another paradox of reality is that the truth is very simple, and yet it also seems to be very complex, particularly when we consider the enormity of its expression. And both of those perceptions are true. Now, that word "perception" is very important. I learned its importance through my studies with Buckminster Fuller, who taught me that every event, or experience, has a minimum of twelve viewpoints. That's a fact which I've been promising for years to demonstrate.

So, let's take a look at some of what Bucky called Energetic/Synergetic Geometry. For the next half dozen pages we will be examining some of the basic principles of geometry. These principles are as good as divine for they apply, without fail, in every given circumstance of equal possibilities. The simplest example of this would be that if we take one of anything and add to it one of the same thing, the result is that we have two of that "thing." One plus one equals two. We might just as well say that one plus one **always** equals two. When we add one and one, the result is always two.

By examining a few basic geometric principles, we will discover certain numbers that are familiar to us from cultural and religious usage. Looking at these numbers from a geometric perspective can help us to better understand the underlying reason for their importance.

Now perhaps you may not think that you like math and geometry. I know that it can be pretty dry. However, I've got a take, and an approach, that will probably be new for most readers. You may find that it will make geometry come alive for you. So I invite you **not** to jump ahead to page 119. I'm certain, however, that you will do what you will.

Through our geometric examination we will discover why God is a trinity, and then further discover what our next perception of God will be beyond the trinity. We'll also find out why there are a minimum of twelve perceptual viewpoints to every expression and therefore why there were twelve disciples.

We want to begin with an event, an expression of principle. All experience is due to our experience, through perception, of the effects and results of the expression of principle. God is that principle, perceived, by us, as principles. Geometry has discovered many of those principles and placed them together in an orderly manner. Let's take a look at that order.

In the beginning is the idea, taking form through the word, moving through expression into manifestation. That creative expression is omni-directional. Think of that expression as manifesting, or emanating, from an individual invisible point. "Point" is the word that geometry uses for the origin of what we're talking about here. I prefer to call it an "event." We're merely using two different words, or perceptions, for the same reality.

Initially that omni-directional expansive expression is equally expressive in all directions. However, as it impacts with the expansive expression of other events which are coming into expression through the word from divine idea, it begins to take a form which is unique to its experience of expression. But if we consider this emerging event before any of those impacts occur, it will appear as a sphere, a three-dimensional 360 degree all-directional circle.

The radius of a circle or a sphere is the distance from its center to its outer circumference or surface. For the sake of example I'm going to speak of that radius as being one unit. That unit can be whatever you choose in your view or perception, but the idea here is that the radii of all events in this example are equal to one of whatever, so it's one unit - of whatever.

Radius--->

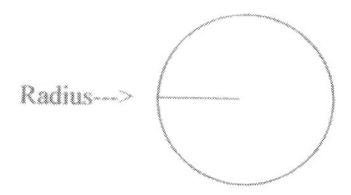

So here I have a model of an expanding event with unit radius one. If I add a second event of unit radius one and place them so that they touch one another in their omni-directional expression, that place at which they first experience one another, they will look like this.

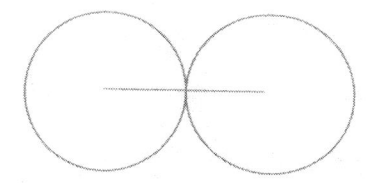

Now that we have a second event, we can add an additional way of viewing the relationship between them by connecting their centers, those points of creation from which they both emanate. In Geometry, this is called a line. It is a straight line because a straight line is the most economical way of making that connection between two points, or two events. It is the shortest distance between the events. Any deviation to straight lengthens the line and alters the perception.

So we now have two events impinging upon one another and the most economically efficient connection between those two events is a line. That line additionally represents perception. Of course, since there are two events involved here, the line really represents two perceptions, each of the other, and shortly I'll show you how we can model that. And for the benefit of accounting, the length of our example "line" is two units (or radii).

Now, what geometry refers to as a line, I prefer to call a vector. A vector, rather than being a thing, specifies direction. The line is not real. Its only reality is in the relationship created by the impingement of the expression of the two events. The line therefore represents the direction of that relationship. For the sake of simplicity, it is an economical straight vector. Our perception here is one dimensional. It only has the dimension of length. It has no width or depth.

Now, let's add a third radiating event. Here things begin to take on a whole new reality. We now have three events, three spheres of expression. And the number of relationships or vectors of perception between them is three. Furthermore, a new player has entered the field, for these three events, or these three perspectives, define a new entity, the combined relationship between them.

Geometry refers to that new entity as a plane. I prefer to refer to it as an appearance. We now have the most basic shape in the universe of appearances. It is called a triangle. And no matter where you place the three events which define this appearance, the appearance will always be a triangle, a shape with three sides, though its shape will vary in respect to the different relationships, or perspectives, which are created as these events shift location.

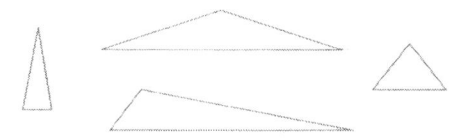

A further enhancement to our modeling has been added because we are now in two dimensions, wherein our basic shape triangle has length and width. This length and width may be measured in a multitude of ways as long as the measurement remains in the two-dimensional appearance.

Now, my dear friends, what we have here is a model of the God of the Christian Church, as determined by the Council of Nicaea 326 CE, over three hundred years after the ministry of Jesus. This is God at its most basic on a level at which we can understand it. The trinity. Father, Son and Holy Ghost. Or, as Dr. H. Emilie Cady expresses it in her book, *Lessons In Truth*, (which has long been referred to as Unity's basic textbook): "mind, idea, and expression." I have chosen to refer to this trinity as comprised of events, vectors (of perception), and appearance (or face). Classic geometry calls them points, lines, and a plane. These are all merely names, designed to define these expressions of principles.

Does it occur to you that there is something wrong with this perception of God? It appears to me that it is confined to being only two-dimensional. No matter where one locates the three events which define our triangle, they always reside in a plane of two dimensions. Our model shows the 3 vectors of perspective that are created by closest packing of 3 events.

Let's now see what happens when we add a fourth event to our model. If we add it so that it is packed closest to the other three events, we discover the shape of the tetrahedron, the smallest, most economical, most basic shape of three-dimensional universe.

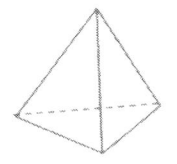

And we see that something new has appeared here. Instead of adding one more vector of perception, we have added three vectors, doubling the previous number. And these vectors now define four appearances or faces, instead of just one. Furthermore, they have created a new entity, the area bounded by their events, vectors, and appearances. I think of this three-dimensional space as expression. Geometry would call this a solid. However, we see that it is not solid at all. It comes into creation through the perceptions of relationships between events in expression. I call it reality, as we know it, in its simplest form. It is the most efficient, minimal reality of three-dimensional experience. Science calls this a tetrahedron.

So our model of expression as a three-dimensional tetrahedron shows us that the expression is defined by at least six vectors of perception. Now, what comes next is truly amazing. If we consider moving beyond the third dimension to the fourth dimension, physicists tell us that in the fourth dimension it is possible to turn physical objects inside out. It's kind of like creating a completely inverted mirror image. If we do that with our tetrahedron, the result will look like this (think of the left as the original and the right as the inverted fourth dimensional mirror copy).

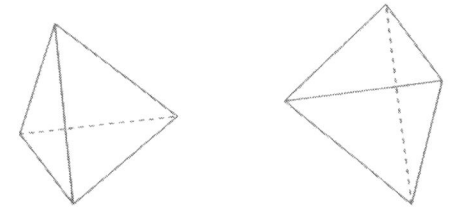

Every event, every vector, every appearance has an opposite. It's important to remember that there is no right or wrong involved here. Everything simply is.

Next, if we then merge our two tetrahedrons together, since they are complementary to one another, we get something that looks like this. Buckminster Fuller called this a star tetrahedron. We can also think of it as the basic model of unitary experience.

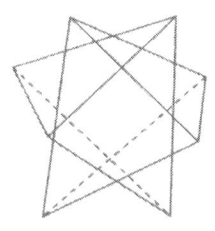

This fourth-dimensional model of a star tetrahedron provides us with eight events expressing a minimum of twelve vectors of perception surrounding a unique experience. Hear me: unique expression of experience is surrounded by a minimum twelve vectors of perception (disciples). And therein we discover the geometric foundation of the structural ministry of Jesus.

One final thought before we move on. If our geometric modeling, which is founded totally upon mathematical principles of God, principles of the entire universe, is considered to be the basic model of God in "three" dimensions as a tetrahedron, then what do you suppose the fourth event which moved the divine trinity into the third dimension would be called? I have my own thoughts on that matter, but for now I'd just like to throw the question out there for the consideration of all. Sometimes it's good not to have all of the answers, otherwise self-discovery is stifled. So, think about it: Father, Son, Holy Ghost and what? Mind, idea, expression and what?

The individual viewpoint which each of us chooses when we apprehend and comprehend an experience is our perception. It is our belief construct about the experience. You may recall that in the Introduction I referred to R. D. Laing, and his book, *Politics of Experience,* in which he helps us to understand that our experiences are totally unique to each and every one of us. Furthermore, we cannot truly share an experience because of the uniqueness of that very experience. That implies that every event potentially contains an infinite multitude of experiences, for each unique consciousness, or aspect of universal consciousness, which apprehends the event experiences it differently. So, we see that every event can be singular, and yet, through the potential of experience, it can be infinite.

One of the puzzles of the creation of the United States of America is how to interpret the phrase in the Declaration of Independence that "all men are created equal." That equality is an expression of the potentiality contained within our source of being. We are all equal in the oneness of our possibilities. If, at our core, as Deepak Chopra says, we are a field of all possibilities, then we share an equality of potential with everyone else. Yet the content and the expression of those possibilities are totally unique.

I have used the term "singularity" to identify this oneness. It is a term which I ran across in the book, *9 ½ Mystics,* a book about Cabala, or Jewish Mysticism by Herbert Weiner. You are a singularity, a totally unique expression of God. As such, you are very special. In that specialty that you are, there is no comparison with anyone or anything else. You are no better and no worse than any other expression of God. And that goes for everyone, whether it is Adolph Hitler or Mother Teresa or a child dying of starvation. We are each a unique expression of God, and because our source is good, the expression of our being is perfect, in spite of all appearances.

Now, the results might not measure up. That happens when we lose track of the truth of who and what we are, when we turn our backs upon the truth of the reality of the singularity and the source of its being. We are perfect, divine beings, but if we do not allow that truth to express through us, from the core of our singularity, but instead we refuse to allow its full flow through us by using the limitation of our choice and our judgments, then we may well create disruptive results. The results of our actions, our conscious allowance of how much of spirit expresses through us, can likewise generate results, which, in this world of appearance take on the guise of punishments. If we limit how much good expresses in our lives, we are bound to suffer.

We have group, or cultural, punishments, and we also have individual, personal punishments which are of our own making. But we should always remember that in this world of appearance, that all is precisely that, appearance. No matter how real the appearance, it is still an appearance.

We are now in a world in which we have created computer generated realities which we refer to as virtual reality. In virtual reality, experiences are created through feeding data to our brains which give the impression of a reality as we have defined it. These realities are not really real. They only appear to be real. That's why they are called virtual, because they appear to be so real that we believe that they are real. Are they real? Well, they are real for the one experiencing them. So they are real. But for those not experiencing them, they are not real, at least not in the same sense as for those directly experiencing them.

It's like when I was in the Navy and was stationed on Midway Island. One night in the barracks at 3 a.m. we were awakened by this incredibly bizarre noise. We didn't know at first what was going on, what was causing this racket. But a quick run through the barracks to the source revealed a hilarious scene. There, in a small cubicle, a sailor was sitting on the floor, cross legged, with a set of headphones on. And, at the top of his voice, not realizing how loud his voice was, he was "singing along" with the song that he was listening to. The song was "In A Gadda Da Vida," by the Iron Butterfly, and not only was he singing loud and extremely out of tune, but it was obvious that he didn't know many of the words and merely substituted mumbled sounds in their place.

He thought that he was singing along with the Iron Butterfly. We, on the other hand, thought that he was being skinned alive. Two separate views of reality, of the world of appearance. Both were right. Neither one was right. It's all a matter of personal perspective.

Don't get fooled by appearances. You are a unique expression of God. You are absolutely, totally, uniquely, singularly, exquisitely, fully God in expression. Everything you think, feel, say, and do is God in expression.

Now you might not feel that to be true, but that's merely your perspective at the moment. Change your perspective and you'll change the results which are the appearances by which so many of us make our judgments about what we think is real and what is not real.

Being an expression of God means that God has created you, uniquely, as a way of expressing itself. You are therefore special. You are special like a child is to a parent. This is why God is often referred to as Father. I sometimes prefer to use the term Father-Mother, to include the all-encompassing expression of this parental feeling of God toward its creation. God created you to express itself. And God gave you the freedom and the power of choice to choose how much of God is going to express through you and the ways in which it is going to express itself.

And then you were given, through creation, the ability of perception, to experience that which is expressing in, around, and through you. You are like a feedback to God of its expression. You are therefore a channel of expression and a channel of experience. The flow runs both ways. God is not only expressing through you, but also is using you to experience that expression of itself. That's a double responsibility for us, for we not only determine how God expresses through us but we also determine how we will report the experience of that expression back to God.

Do you understand why you are a singularity, why you are important, why you are truly a child of God, made in God's image and God's likeness, and therefore are also a divine creator? Each of us is creating our own reality, through our choices and our expressions and our experiences and our perceptions. The sum total of all of those unique realities is God's feedback and every single bit is just as important as any other bit.

Virtual reality is really nothing new. We've all been doing it our entire lives. Once we realize the truth of that reality and more fully comprehend the importance of our singularity, then we can begin to alter our reality in whatever ways we choose. Some people choose not to believe that. Their reality, therefore, does not contain that option, but that option does not exist for them merely because they refuse to believe it, not because it isn't so.

Jesus was a unique expression of God who consciously made contact with the Christ perfection within himself, the field of all possibilities, and he allowed that Christ to express through him in a way which has affected, and continues to affect, billions of people through his example.

You are also a unique expression of God, and you are making conscious contact with the Christ perfection within yourself, that field of all possibilities, and allowing that Christ to express through you in whatever ways you choose to let it express through the choice of your beliefs.

Become still. Think about the breath of God, the breath of life, being blown into your nostrils at this very moment. What a special gift. What a unique opportunity. It won't last forever. Don't let it go to waste. Begin living life like the unique singularity that you are. Today is the best time there is to start.

To fully comprehend that truth, while in this still moment of contemplation, consciously connect with that Christ within you and consciously choose to allow it fuller expression in your life from here on out.

Meditate on this reality: **I Am now in the presence of pure being and fully open to the unique expression of my Christ self.**

Next, we'll examine what happens when we turn our back on the reality of our singularity.

ULTIMATE SIN IS DENIAL OF THE TRUTH

To question or doubt the divinity of our singularity is the ultimate sin of denial; it is denying the existence of, and the full and complete expression of, God.

ULTIMATE SIN IS DENIAL OF THE TRUTH

Well, we have talked about the infinity of God's expression by realizing the incredible, special, individual uniqueness of each one of us. I like to call that "specialness you" that you are, and the "specialness I" that I am, the singularity. Three chapters ago we identified that uniqueness that each of us is as stemming directly from God. And we explained that our relationship to our creator has a special closeness similar to that between a parent and a child.

The institutional "churchianity" part of the Christian experience down through the centuries tried to take that individual spiritual uniqueness which each of us shares and make it an exclusive experience to Jesus and Jesus only. It was not the intention of Jesus that this should be a part of the teachings passed down from his ministry. That is why the early church organizers argued for several hundred years among themselves before the "only begotten" faction won out over the "all are God's creation" group.

I point these things out because many people have no clue about how the "church" developed its beliefs and rituals and traditions. A little insight into the origins of these matters often helps to bring a greater personal clarity to our understanding of our true nature and the teachings of Jesus and other master teachers. Many of the important foundation stones of the Christian church did not have their official beginning until decades, or even centuries after Jesus' crucifixion.

For example, God didn't become a trinity until the fourth century C.E. (AD). That is when that concept was officially embraced by the church and became a part of official doctrine. The idea of the fall of man and original sin is not a part of the actual text of the Torah (first five books of the Old Testament or Jewish Bible). Although the text has remained the same, the twist of the fall, and evil sex, and God's curse weren't added as official **interpretations** until long after the apostles were all dead and gone. Most people are not even aware that the early church (we're talking about the first 500 years here) once had a meeting of Bishops and other church leaders to decide whether or not women are human. Fortunately, women secured their claim to humanity by a single vote. I don't know what would have happened if they would have had hanging chads back then.

The church is, by nature and by definition, an institution. It is not a person. It is not a creation of God. It is a creation of mankind, and like all of humanity's creations, it is open to improvement. In fact, it begs for improvement. Think of something, anything, that you've ever created. Don't you know that you could have done it better if given a second chance? That's because we are constantly learning in our doing. Well, life is like that because we are not God. We are, rather, creations of God. We are manifestations of God. As God's creations, we are constantly growing and changing and unfolding in all aspects of our "being." Physically, mentally, emotionally, intellectually, spiritually, relationally, we are evolving (I don't always like that word because of its connections to Darwinism, but it is what is happening individually and collectively in our lives). We, you and I, are growing. We, all of us, are growing. And when that growth ceases in this physical apparatus that we currently inhabit, then we shake the dust from our sandals and move onward in our continued infinite growth.

But the organized church threw a monkey wrench in the works. They declared, many years after Jesus made his departure from this physical plane, that Jesus was "special." He was a trick baby. He wasn't the same as the rest of us. He was different. He was THE son of God. Well, you know what that did to the rest of us: it made us subservient to HIS successor, the organized church. Jesus spoke of a church being built upon faith, but instead the church built itself upon the condemnation and fear that are the tools of power.

Attention, people. This was **not** Jesus' intention. He did not imply that he was different or better than us. He did not intend that we should believe that he had a different relationship with our creator than we have. The apparent differences between Jesus and ourselves have their foundation in each person's awareness of the truth about themselves and their willingness to allow those truths to express in their lives and affairs. It has nothing to do with supernatural magic in an attempt to circumvent the laws of God.

Jesus did NOT claim to be the only begotten of God. Whoever wrote the book of John made that claim for him. How could I say that about the author of the book of John? Because it is only in the book of John that we find Jesus making "I am" statements. "I am the way, the truth, and the life..." "I am the light of the world..." "I am the vine, you are the branches..." "I am the bread of life." "I am the good shepherd ..." "I am not of this world ..." You won't find those statements in the book of Matthew. Look in Mark. You won't find them there either. Luke? Again, the answer is no. Jesus is not reported as having made any of these glorified "I am" statements which would appear to place him in a position somewhere above and/or separate and apart from us. Such statements are only found in the gospel of John. That's why I claim a unique agenda was generated from the author of John.

In fact, the book of John was not accepted for several centuries by the church. When the church finally decided to incorporate John into the "official" accepted teaching, then John's unique take on Jesus and his ministry were used by members of the church hierarchy to create the belief that Jesus was different, that he was God made flesh, while the rest of us are merely made from the dust. In John 3:16, it is the author of John who claims Jesus as being the "only begotten" of God. It is not Jesus speaking.

Further examination of that verse reveals interesting commentary. Regarding translation from the Greek, *McCord's New Testament Translation of the Everlasting Gospel"* contains the following footnote: "The word 'begotten' in John 1: 14, 18; 3: 16, 18;

Hebrews 11: 17; 1 John 4: 9 is eliminated (1) for the sake of accuracy and (2) for the sake of the honor that belongs to Isaac and to Jesus. .... . In none of the six citations mentioned above did the infallible Holy Spirit cause monos gennetheis, only begotten, to be written, but in every instance the word written is monogenes, the only one of a kind, the unique one."

Likewise, in looking at the original Aramaic, we discover in Dr. Rocco Errico's book, *Let There Be Light,* http://www.noohra.com that "yeheedaya, does not mean 'only-begotten.' It means 'sole,' 'only,' 'precious,' 'beloved,' and the 'one of a kind.' This word also, by implication, refers to the 'firstborn son.'" Dr. Errico's book reveals much more for those interested in pursuing the subject. The bottom line here is that Jesus is divine, but for the same reasons that each of us is divine, for we were all created by God in God's image and likeness.

As we stated several chapters ago, we agree with Paul when he said, in his letter to the church at Corinth, "the mystery hidden from ages" is "Christ in you, your hope of glory." And that Christ expresses in an infinite number of ways. I have chosen to refer to each of those divine, unique, individual, infinite ways as a singularity. You are, therefore, a divine singularity.

Now, the seventh statement in our series is: **To question or doubt the divinity of our singularity is the ultimate sin of denial; it is denying the existence of, and the full and complete expression of, God.**

The true definition of the word, "sin," is to miss the mark. The way in which Jesus dealt with sin, time and time again, was to advise the "sinner" to "stop doing it." No "hail Marys," no "our Fathers," no self-flagellation, just repent and "don't do it again." And what does "repent" mean? It means to turn to God. How simple can it get? Turn your attention back to the awareness of God and your connection to

God as God in expression and stop doing that which caused you to sin, to miss the mark.

The biggest mark which we can miss is the mark of accepting our own divinity. You are a child of God. You are therefore an heir to the kingdom of God. There's really no two ways about that. You can deny it if you choose. You can hide from the truth of those statements. You can run. But no matter what you do, you can't get away from that gut feeling that what we're talking about here is really the truth.

And isn't this what Jesus was saying when his disciples asked him (Matthew 22:36-40) what was the greatest commandment and he responded, "Love the Lord your God with all your heart and with all your soul and with all your might and with all your mind. This is the greatest and the first commandment. And the second is like to it, Love your neighbor as yourself." Yep. Repent and sin no more. Couldn't get much simpler.

Several years ago I learned the **Lord's Prayer** in Ancient Aramaic from Dr. Rocco Errico. Like Dr. Errico, I now open all of my classes and services with this prayer, as reportedly spoken by Jesus, in his native tongue. And to keep that as a regular part of my consciousness I always pray that prayer aloud every time I take I shower. Sort of an internal and an external cleansing at the same time. The prayer begins, "Awoon," also spelled "Awon" or "Abwoon" in English. That word means "Our Father." It is not, "My Father." It is "Our Father." It is not singular; it is plural. Jesus introduces the prayer with these words,

> *When you pray, do not be like the hypocrites, who like to pray, standing in the synagogues and at the street corners, so that they may be seen by men. Truly I say to you that they have already received their reward.*

> But as for you, when you pray, enter into your inner chamber and lock your door, and pray to your Father who is in secret, and your Father who sees in secret shall himself reward you openly.
>
> And when you pray, do not repeat your words like the pagans, for they think that because of much talking they will be heard.
>
> Do not be like them, for your Father knows what you need, before you ask him;
>
> Therefore pray in this manner; Our Father ...

And you know the rest. But he doesn't talk about "my" Father. He speaks, and this is to thousands during the "Sermon on the Mount," of "your" Father. And then begins the suggested prayer itself with, "Our Father." I don't see how our oneness, our brotherhood and sisterhood with Jesus, and therefore with one another, could be clearer. Our Father. We are all God's children.

As I have already stated, my mother taught me that every conception is Immaculate. God is present and fully active in every single conception, whether the active participants are aware of it or not. There is no need to try to turn it into something supernatural. The entire process is already naturally super.

We're talking in this chapter about the divinity of our singularity. Do you know what I mean by that? The divinity of our singularity? It means that each of us is an absolutely unique and special child, a unique creation, of God.

Now, we have a bit of a paradox here. Since God is all there is, and God is all good, then there can't really be any part of the expression of God that is any better than any other part. There's an incredible equality, a unity throughout all of creation. So from that standpoint we cannot make the claim of being special. Yet, because each of us is unique, therefore we are special. That's what the singularity is all about. It's the special uniqueness of expression that each of us is within the equality of God's manifestation.

We have talked about how each of us is a unique expression of God, and how, since God is all there is and God is all good, we are each therefore all good. Furthermore, we have already discussed the fact that evil does not exist since God is all good.

Now we find the question of sin needing to be addressed. I'm going to give you another paradox to digest here. First, I'm going to explain why there is no sin. Then I'm going to explain what sin is, in the context of what is known as original sin, and why it came into being, even though it doesn't exist.

No, this is not a magic show. There's no sleight of hand. I'm merely examining the facts and reporting what I find. In the process we are discovering an understanding of things as they are which is beyond the normal linear concept of what we call reality.

In this book I have emphasized that there are a minimum of twelve different viewpoints for every experience in universe. I am merely, therefore, sharing another viewpoint, albeit one that is grounded and makes an increasing amount of sense.

In the Garden of Eden story in Genesis, we find Adam man and Eve man apparently getting bored with frolicking in the woods and working for God as a gardener and his helpmate. I refer to both Adam and Eve as man for they are representative of humanity as a created whole.

As Charles Fillmore says in the *The Metaphysical Bible Dictionary*, "Adam is the first movement of mind in its contact with life and substance. Adam also represents the generic man, or the whole human race epitomized in an individual-man idea. Eve is the feminine aspect of generic man, outwardly manifest: 'male and female created he them.'"

Now, you may remember that I pointed out that last phrase, taken from the first chapter of Genesis, before the creation of Adam and Eve and said that it could be interpreted as meaning that each and every human being is both male and female, though each in varying degrees upon various levels. Since Eve, the feeling nature, is a major player in Chapter Three of Genesis, let's see what Fillmore has to say about Eve:

> *Love, or feeling, in individual consciousness. The I AM (wisdom) puts feeling into what it thinks, and so "Eve" (feeling) becomes the "mother of all living." Feeling is Spirit, which quickens. Woman symbolizes the soul region of man and is the mother principle of God in expression. Back of the woman (feeling) is the pure life essence of God. Adam and Eve represent the I AM identified in life substance. They are the primal elemental forces of Being itself.*

So it is our feeling nature that gets tempted, or otherwise coerced by the serpent to eat of the one tree which she and Adam, our intellect, were told to leave alone. And that sets the stage for the ongoing battle between our intellect and our feeling nature.

You know, if God didn't want them to mess with the tree, why did God bother to say anything about it? It sounds as though God might have set them/us up. Them/us? Of course. Adam and Eve are representative of all of humanity, both on a total basis and as individuals. This is, therefore, your story. Or, as Ralph Edwards used to say, "This is your life!" By God identifying this tempting tree of the knowledge of good and evil, humanity has been set up, through its innate, God-given curiosity, to choose to eat of the fruit of the tree. And the consequences be damned.

Since we have so many trees playing important parts in this chapter, the Tree of Life, the Tree of the Knowledge of Good and Evil, and the trees behind which Adam and Eve hide from God after eating the fruit and discovering their nakedness, let's look at these metaphysical trees.

Trees? Well, again, we'll let Charles tell us.

"Trees" represent nerves, and nerves are expressions of thoughts of unity; they connect thought centers.

The "tree" (Gen. 2:9) signifies the connecting link between earth and heaven - between body and mind, the formless and the formed. 'Every tree that is pleasant to the sight' pertains to the perceptive faculty of mind. It is always pleasant to perceive Truth. The substance of spiritual thought is the "food" that is good. The "tree of life also in the midst of the garden" represents the absolute life principles established in man consciousness by Divine Mind. The roots of the tree of life are centered in the solar plexus region, and they are symbolized in the physical organism by the nerves.

The generative center in the loins of man is the point at which the physical man contacts life, but when the consciousness has been redeemed and man has placed himself in the "garden" through I AM, Jehovah God, he contacts the "tree of life" at the solar plexus region, or heart center, and from this center exercises authority and dominion over the whole current of life in the organism.

The "tree of the knowledge of good and evil" represents the discerning capacity of mind. Man first perceives Truth; then he must discern the relation of ideas before perfect activity is set up within him.

Jehovah God told Adam to avoid the tree whose fruit was a knowledge of good and evil, "for in the day that thou eatest thereof thou shalt surely die." It is evident that this tree is closely related to individual free will, which is in direct touch with the "serpent" or selfhood. In that state of consciousness, or day, the individual shall surely die.

The branch that separates itself from the tree withers away and dies. So a belief by the ego that its life, substance, and intelligence are self-derived cuts off the source of supply, and the ego begins to revolve in a mental vortex whose dominant tones are good and evil, birth and death - duality.

It is through the affections, the feminine in us, that we partake of both good and evil. The soul, or woman, was given to man by Jehovah God, and is the avenue through which the inspirations of Spirit come. When the I AM assumes mastery over the soul it brings forth only good.

If man could lay hold of the tree of life while thinking both good and evil to be real, he would go on living in the negative part of his being and would bring destruction upon himself.

Man lost consciousness of his divine nature in Spirit, and so must begin again to lay hold of the potential ideas in substance and must till the ground from whence he was taken.

So, having been introduced to the tree, Adam and Eve, that's right, they are together when all of this takes place, they allow the serpent, the self-absorbed ego, to entice them into partaking of the knowledge of good and evil.

We'll look at just what this knowledge of good and evil is, but first let's see what Charles has to say about the serpent:

> The "serpent" of the garden of Eden is sense consciousness. It may also be called desire, and sensation, or the activity of life in an external expression, apart from the Source of life.

So the serpent is our sense consciousness, that part of us which is tuned in to the appearances as dominating forces in our life. The appearance is such a temptation to our senses, that we make the mistake of thinking that the appearance is the source, is the essence itself. But it is only the appearance. And that appearance can change, and it can be altered by us through the choices of our egoistic perceptions.

In light of the data received by our senses, we choose to think that, unlike the reality of God, there appears to be good and evil, right and wrong; in other words we establish a belief in the reality of duality, that there can be, that there is, something other than God.

We think that this is what God can do and that by doing the same, that makes us equal with God. We are not equal with God, no matter what we may choose to think. However, we are God, even though we are not equal to God. Now if all of this keeps sounding very deep, or complex, or contradictory, that's because the "wisdom of God is foolishness" in our eyes.

The true reality is beyond our comprehension. And that's particularly true of our senses; our senses have no possibility whatsoever in actually comprehending the reality of God. That is not what they are designed to do. They are designed to be the source of data in our world of appearance.

So, as with Adam and Eve, we grow up relying upon the report of our senses and we then believe it to be the totality of reality, thus separating us, by our own choice, from the truth of our being, that we are children of God, and heirs to all good. This is the divinity of our singularity. To question that fact, to doubt or disbelieve it, is committing the ultimate sin of denying the truth, the truth about God and the truth about ourselves.

This story of Genesis Chapter Three is often told as if God were a demanding, judging, punishing God. But that is not so. Remember it said "the LORD God made for Adam and for his wife coats of skin, and clothed them."

Whew, as I am pulling these ideas together, I am asking myself, "what kind of skin?" And one possible answer is the skin of physical humanity. In other words, could this line mean that it was not until the singularity eats of the tree of the knowledge of good and evil that it actually takes on physical visibility? There's a thought for you. For those who like to "take the Bible literally," it literally says in Genesis that God clothed us with skin. It says what it says. It is what it is.

Anyway, this is a loving God, a loving parent. When the child shows shame for its nakedness, the parent creates clothes to cover that nakedness. The parent doesn't further shame the child for being ashamed. There's no blame game here.

Then because of man's knowledge of good and evil and in light of the fact that man might next seek immortality, God sends him out of the garden to work on another piece of ground. Man must leave the garden now that he perceives good and evil because that is a reality that is not of the garden.

Then it says God "drove the man out." As an aside here, for those who like to interpret the Bible literally, I ask what kind of car or vehicle God drove the man out in, and was Adam's wife, Eve, driven out with him? Or did she have to walk.

Anyway, once outside, Cherubim are placed at the east of the garden with a flaming sword to guard the path to the tree of life. What are the cherubim? They are symbolic of Divine Mind. It is therefore through meditation upon spiritual thoughts, rather than the world of appearance, that we can regain entry to the garden.

So, in this allegory we see that the sin of man is in not seeing the whole picture, it is in judging by appearances and thereby believing that which only appears to be, rather than that which is, and is by its very nature, beyond the limitations of appearance. Of course, the organized church, with its emphasis on form, ritual, tradition, and dogma encourages a world view constructed around the duality of appearances.

It is in our choosing to cease living our lives based upon sense appearance and instead basing our lives upon spiritual principle, and following up that choice with a life focused upon regular meditation and practice of truth principles that we can break out of the dream of sense appearance and begin to return to the garden which is our birthright.

Now I'd like to share with you Dr. Rocco Errico's commentary upon this chapter of Genesis. This is from his book, *Let There Be Light: The Seven Keys.*

> *At some time in the tenth century B.C.E., a Hebrew scribe penned the famous legend of Adam and Eve. In the book of Genesis it follows the prose poem of creation. Most of the time this ancient literary piece suffers from improper*

and negative interpretations that are mistaken notions about the meaning of the narrative. This narrative has often been viewed as dealing with "The Fall of Man," "Original Sin," "The Origin of Evil," "The Origin of Death," and "The Evils of Sexual Union."

Knowledgeable Hebrew Scripture experts and scholars of ancient Near Eastern history no longer hold these so-called theological ideas as tenable. But one must avoid the mistake of viewing this "original sin" in terms of a universal and abstract notion of sin. Such a concept is not found in the Old Testament. This notion is Church doctrine and became part of Christian beliefs.

Again, we must keep in mind that the narrative is a Torah parable. It is not a description of history. The Semitic writer, through his tale, tells how the first couple nearly achieve immortality for humankind. Nevertheless, since they did not gain immortality for humanity, they did find something else. They obtained knowledge --- for a price.

Another point to consider is the narrative's ancient Near Eastern setting with its common religious idea and motifs. Although no historian has found any parallel story to the Adam and Eve narrative, the Hebrew account does share familiar themes with certain Ugarit, Canaanite, and Mesopotamian tales. Immortality and knowledge (wisdom) were the major themes recorded in these primitive myths and legends. The author of Genesis 2-3 describes the two common Eastern motifs in metaphoric language. He calls them the 'tree of life' and the 'tree of the knowledge of good and evil.'

Another mistaken notion is the cursing scene. Did the Lord God curse Adam and Eve for their transgression?

Does all humanity suffer because of the misdeed of these two individuals? Upon whom did God put a curse?

"The Lord [Yahweh] God said to the serpent: Concerning this thing you have done, cursed are you among all cattle, and among all wild animals; on your belly shall you slither, and dust shall you eat your whole life long. . . . To the woman he said: I will increase greatly your pains in childbearing, in pain you shall be dependent upon your husband and he shall rule over you. . . Then to the man he said. . . . cursed is the ground because of you. . . ."

As you can see from the above passages of Scripture, Yahweh God did not curse the woman or the man. God only put a curse on the serpent and the ground. The idea of the wife's position as dependent upon her husband is not a punishment. The subordinate position of the wife had to do with the social customs of the times. This verse explains women's social status after the fact. It did not create the status; it only confirms it. And, to embellish his tale, the writer adds the idea of pain during pregnancy and birth as penalties.

Nevertheless, according to the latest biblical findings and scholarly research, verses 14-19 in Chapter Three were not a part of the original structure of the legend. In an older form of the tale, expulsion from the garden followed right after Yahweh God discovered their disobedience and heard their defense. Exile from Eden was the original and only penalty placed on the man and the woman. The penalties mentioned in verses 14-19 have no direct relationship to the offense that they had committed. What these verses factually describe is the present state of existence of the serpent, woman, and man. And, by way of after-thought, the Torah author or scribe added them as further penalties. It accurately describes existential challenges present in living as human beings on this earth.

So Rocco is telling us that we have a very simple story, a narrative legend, which was embellished thousands of years ago, possibly in copying. Remember that stories were originally passed verbally, rather than in written form. It was the expedient thing to do. There were no mechanical printing devices other than the human hand. And we all know how a story can change with the repeated telling.

Now, Rocco deals with the "Vilification of Women" as represented in this overly embellished Biblical text (again from his book, *Let There Be Light*):

Did the Lord (Yahweh) God curse Eve? Was Eve a temptress? And was she ultimately responsible for all the woes and difficulty that humanity faces today? Let us examine more closely the verses and assumptions that stem from this famous tale. Remember, this is a sacred story that conveys certain ideas. It is a Near Eastern parable, not a report.

The view that this tale establishes women in a basically temptress role is grossly inaccurate. The thought that God cursed all women because a woman ate some fruit from a forbidden tree is another fallacious perception. Truly, these notions have become exceedingly harmful religious interpretations of biblical text. Hebrew Scripture does not portray Eve as a temptress:

"So when the woman saw that the tree was good for food, and that it was pleasing to the eyes, and that the tree was delightful to look at, she took the fruit of it, and did eat, and she also gave to her husband with her, and he did eat."

Note that the verse says "she also gave to her husband with her." Evidently, Adam was present and watching the scene between the "woman" and the "serpent."

There is also another clue that points to the fact that Adam was with the "woman" during the alluring conversation with the serpent. In the original Semitic text (both Aramaic and Hebrew) the serpent uses the plural form when addressing the woman. "And the serpent said to the woman, You [pl.---tmuaton] absolutely shall not die; for God knows that in the day you [pl.---aton] eat of it, your eyes shall be opened and you [pl.---aton] shall become like God knowing everything." The story makes it clear that both the man and the woman made the decision to eat the forbidden fruit.

"Original Sin" as an article of Church creed also contributed to the erroneous and horrendous notion that women, by nature, are maleficent. During the Middle Ages it helped instigate an unbelievable vilification of women. It made her the authoress of death and all earthly woe.

Judaism instead of teaching the "Fall of Man," teaches the "Rise of Man"; and instead of "Original Sin," it stresses "Original Virtue." The term "Original Virtue" means the beneficent hereditary influence of righteous ancestors upon their descendants. It also teaches that all children are destined to help in the establishment of God's kingdom on earth.

Interestingly, some Christian Bible teachers call attention to the point that Jesus never refers to 'Original Sin' or to the so-called "Fall of Man." We have no mention in the gospels of the "Fall of Man." What we do find in the gospels is Jesus encouraging his followers to become like children so that they might enter the kingdom of heaven. If children are "born in sin," why would Jesus teach his disciples to become like them?

Thank you, Rocco, for that excellent clarification.

All of this stuff about "original sin" and the "fall of man" distracts us from the real truth of our being. You will recall that in Chapter Four I declared that there is no evil. Well, now I'm going to share with you the fact that there is only one sin. Yes, you heard me correctly. One. And only one. Now, which one do you think it is? Lust? Gluttony? Greed? Sloth? Wrath? Envy? Pride? Oh, and let's not forget Deceit and Fear.

Where did all of these "sins" come from? Well, the book of Proverbs, Chapter Six, verses 16-19 list "six things which the Lord hates; yea, the seventh is an abomination to him." They were: "Haughty eyes, a lying tongue, and hands that shed innocent blood. A heart that devises wicked imaginations, feet that are swift in running to mischief. A false witness who speaks lies, and he who sows discord among brothers." Then, in Paul's "Epistle To The Galations", Chapter Five, verses 19-21, Paul lists "the works of the flesh," which he claims "are well known" as "adultery, impunity, and lasciviousness, idolatry, witchcraft, enmity, strife, jealousy, anger, stubbornness, seditions, heresies, envying, murders, drunkenness, revellings, and all such things." Now we're going to come back to Paul's letter shortly, but first I want to finish what the organized church did with the concept of sin.

Next, in the Fourth Century, a monk, named Evagrius Ponticus, lists eight evil thoughts in Latin. In English, they are: gluttony, lust, greed, sorrow, wrath, despair, vainglory and pride. These were further modified in 590 by Pope Gregory, and so on. The church went on developing these shortcomings into quite a lucrative business, ultimately "selling" dispensations to those who have committed these "sins." The protest against this practice is part of what sparked the Protestant Reformation. However, none of the aforementioned "sins" or "works of the flesh" are the sin which I have in mind. Moreover, "None" of these "sins" can exist without first violating the only "true sin" that I'm about to reveal.

Now let's look back at Paul's Epistle to the Church in Galatia. After listing the "works of the flesh" he went on to list "the fruits of the Spirit" as "love, joy, peace, patience, gentleness, goodness, faith, meekness, self-control." Humanity's challenge seems to be how to acquire these "fruits" while avoiding the "flesh works." And Paul tells us precisely how to do that in Galations 5:13-18 when he says:

For, my brethren, you have been called to liberty; only do not use your liberty for an occasion to the things of the flesh, but by love serve one another.

For the whole law is fulfilled in one saying, that is, You shall love your neighbor as yourself.

But if you harm and plunder one another, take heed lest you be consumed one by another.

This I say then: Lead a spiritual life, and you shall never commit the lust of the flesh.

For the flesh craves that which is harmful to the Spirit, and the Spirit opposes the things of the flesh; and the two are contrary to one another, so that you are unable to do whatever you please.

But if you are led by Spirit, you are not under the law.

And with that said, friends, it's quite obvious why they crucified Jesus, imprisoned Paul, and martyred so many of Jesus' followers. **If you are led by Spirit, you are not under the law.**

Years ago I proclaimed myself to be an outlaw. I got the idea for that from a line from Bob Dylan's "Absolutely Sweet Marie" when he says, "to live outside the law, you must be honest." And where does that honesty spring from? Paul says, "you shall love your neighbor as yourself."

But what if you don't really like yourself? Ah, now we're getting down to the nitty gritty. Let's step back to the "Garden" story for a minute. Remember what precipitated Adam and Eve's troubles? Their troubles all began when the desired to eat of the tree of the knowledge of good and evil. And once they ate of the fruit, what happened? Well, they felt naked and ashamed. They tried to hide from God. How ridiculous. How can one hide from God? What would make one consider hiding from God when God is all there is? Simple. **It is the mistaken belief that one is separate and apart from God. And that, my friends, is the ultimate and only true sin.** It is the primo example of missing the mark.

When you know your oneness with God, all things are possible. No matter where you go, or what your surrounding circumstances, you know that you are in the kingdom of God. And you will be beyond the law. For the law was made by those who commit the ultimate sin, and it applies to all of the other ultimate sinners. But for those who know their oneness with God, the only law is love God and love God's creation, or manifestation. As an added note for those who are already outlaws, and for those who desire to become outlaws, life is a lot less stressful if one "abides" by the law (humankind's "laws"). But you'll find that it's a whole new scenario. As an outlaw you abide by the law as a result of intelligent intention rather than out of fear. Same basic result; different motivation; therefore different experience.

So the only true sin is in the belief that we are separate and apart from God. Commit that sin and you open Paul's Pandora's Box of "things of the flesh."

Now, a gentle reminder if one should find that one is a sinner, a non-believer in the fact of their oneness with God. Let's remind ourselves of how Jesus dealt with "sin." Six simple words: Repent; Go And Sin No More. To the point. All inclusive. Extremely powerful. Repent. Turn toward God. That's what repent means: Turn towards God. Then. Go And Sin No More. Don't hang around and brood. Stop it. Quit. And move on.

Wait, what about the blame and shame? No blame. No shame. That kind of stuff is for losers. Why would anyone be foolish enough to try to blame/shame God in expression? It simply is what it is. Recognize the shortcoming, turn toward God and move on.

Now, sometimes I'll be talking with someone about these principles of God, these "techniques" for living in accord with our true being, and they will come back later and say, "Well, I tried it and it doesn't work." Listen up! This is not some sort of test that you or anyone else is administering to God. IT WORKS! Get that straight. The only question is what the hell you are going to do about it. Are you going to do what WORKS in spite of all appearances, or are you going to continue whining about your life? Hmmm! That sounds straight enough to me.

Dear reader, you are an expression of God. How much of God expresses in your life, and the amount of God that expresses, is up to you and your attitude, your beliefs, your actions, and your direction. That's the truth. Anything other than that is the result of either ignorance or out and out lying. And that's the truth. The choice that Adam and Eve made "in the garden" is the same choice that we make every single day. Now pay attention: it is a "choice," not a "fate." It's all about choices, choices that we make every day.

So, rejoice in the spirit of your divinity. You can start simply by smiling, first to yourself, and then to others. Share a kind word, a good deed. Try dedicating each day to the expression of some positive word, positive concept, positive expression. Peace. Joy. Love. Gratitude. Sharing. Happiness. Forgiveness. There's a week's worth of words (7) to get you started.

If you're a child of God, why not begin to consciously act like it. Let God express more fully in your life, your thoughts, and your affairs, one day at a time. And take time each day to go into your inner closet, become very still and listen. Don't talk. Just listen and feel the God that you are in expression.

As Grace Slick said, when she and the Jefferson Airplane took the stage at Woodstock in 1969, "Good morning, people. It's a new dawn."

Choose now to make this life experience count. I know you can do it.

IN THE GARDEN OF EDEN

Our belief in separation from God causes us to lose sight of the Garden of Eden in which we reside; the garden is the full and total infinite expression of God.

IN THE GARDEN OF EDEN

Our belief in separation from God causes us to lose sight of the Garden of Eden in which we reside; the garden is the full and total infinite expression of God.

What is the Garden of Eden? Let's see what Charles Fillmore had to say about that in *The Metaphysical Bible Dictionary."*

> *The Hebrew "Gan-heden" commonly rendered Garden of Eden is a compound of surpassing greatness. The word Gan means any organized sphere of activity, a garden, a body, a world, a universe. The word Heden, Eden, means a time, a season, an age, an eternity, as well as beauty, pleasure, an ornament, a witness. Thus it can be seen that only the most limited and restricted material acceptation would bring this remarkable word down to a small, hedged-in inclosure, a small area somewhere in Asia where the human race first emerged from the dust of this planet.*

The Garden of Eden story is the story of what happens when we turn our back on the truth of our being and instead give power, through our belief, to the world of appearance. As we can imagine, denying our own divinity opens up a Pandora's Box of self-created problems, giving rise to the appearance of evil and evidence of the work of the devil.

The devil/Satan holds an important place in the belief system of many people in the world. It is a place of power, yet it has no power in and of itself. Its sole power comes from the belief of those who believe in it. Charles Fillmore gives us some important insight into the roots of this belief in evil in *The Metaphysical Bible Dictionary* about the devil.

> *The deceiving phase of mind in man that has fixed ideas in opposition to truth (adversary, lier in wait, accuser, opposer, hater, an enemy). Satan assumes various forms in man's consciousness, among which may be mentioned egotism, a puffing up of the personality; and the opposite of this, self-depreciation, which admits the "accuser" into the consciousness. This "accuser" makes man believe that he is inherently evil.*
>
> *Satan is the "Devil," a state of mind formed by man's personal ideas of his power and completeness and sufficiency apart from God. Besides at times puffing up the personality, this satanic thought often turns about and, after having tempted one to do evil, discourages the soul by accusing it of sin. Summed up, it is the state of mind in man that believes in its own sufficiency independent of its creative Source.*

There is a certain aspect of organized religion that teaches that Satan, or the devil, or the incarnation of evil is actually at fault for all of the bad things which happen to us. So, let's deal with that before we examine our relationship to the Garden of Eden. One of my teachers, Alan Stanley, during a Sunday service in Albuquerque, New Mexico, helped me to put the Satan/devil/evil bugaboo to rest once and for all. He did it with a piece of scripture from the book of John, of all places. Don't forget, it is John who is constantly portraying Jesus as one making extravagant personal claims about himself. In spite of that, however, the book of John is a source of a perspective that delves deeper into an understanding of the impact of Jesus' teaching than the superficial view that many people hold about Jesus and his ministry.

So, in the eighth Chapter of John, verses 30-59, John relates the following story. It seems that Jesus is talking with some of his Jewish followers and they begin to question his authority, ultimately leading to their turning on him, which results in Jesus running and hiding.

> *They said to him, We are not born of fornication; we have one Father, God.*

And in verse 42 we read:

> *Jesus said to them, If God were your Father, you would love me.*

In verse 44 Jesus goes on to say:

> *You are from the father of accusation, and you want to do the lusts of your father, he who is a murderer of men from the very beginning and who never stands by the truth, because there is no truth in him. When he speaks he speaks his own lie, because he is a liar, and the father of lies.*

"He is a liar and the father of lies." This scripture tells us that Satan or the devil or the incarnation of evil is actually lies, is the source of lies. It's all lies. It is the father of lies. Satan is a lie. The devil is a lie. Evil is a lie. Lack and limitation are lies. Believing that we are separate and apart from God is a lie. The belief that we reside anywhere other than in the Garden of Eden is a lie.

So here we have the major challenge of life: the battle between the true reality of who we are - creations of God, expressions of God, children of God - and our belief in the lie of our own separate self-importance. It is when we believe ourselves separate and apart from God that we are ruled by our problems. Our problems can seem so big that they appear to take on a personality of their own. When we are aware of our oneness with God, then no problem can affect us. Though all around you the world may seem to be crumbling, yet you remain steadfast in the truth of your being and the comfort which that brings. This truly is residing in the Garden of Eden.

I once had a printed copy from my website of some of the notes for this chapter lying about on my desk. One of the engineers with whom I worked at the time saw some of the notes and said, "That's really deep." I hadn't yet gotten around to rereading the notes myself, but when I did, I had to concur. This is deep. The author of the book of John, and Charles Fillmore, and I had also written some real deep stuff several years earlier.

Now, I don't want that to frighten anyone off. I don't mean that this is deep in an overwhelming sense. What we're going to share here is easily comprehensible by anyone. But it's the ramifications that are incredible, for what our current subject does is to give us a different perspective from which to view our world of reality.

Think for a minute about what life was like for you just 40 years ago, say the 1970's, if you have even been alive that long. Circa 1970, the breakup of the Beatles, Woodstock, walking on the moon, getting into and out of the Vietnam War, Watergate, bell bottoms, Elton John declared the entertainer of the decade at the "beginning" of the decade. No personal computers, no CD's, no DVD's, no Internet, no clones, no Space Shuttles, no cell phones, no cable TV, no genetically engineered food. Got the picture? Okay, now imagine that you lie down to go to sleep back in 1970 or 1971 and you don't wake up again until this morning.

Whoa! Things have changed. Some things have changed dramatically. The changes may seem very deep. But the grass still grows, the flowers still bloom, night and day still follow their usual cycles, people are born, live, fall in love, have babies, raise children, die. That, too, is deep. But the depth in all of it is a matter of perspective. And so it is with this chapter's topic. It can appear deep, but that viewpoint of depth usually occurs if the subject is a radical departure from our usual way of perceiving reality. And although this may be a dramatic change for our frame of reference, I guarantee you that we have the ability to adapt to it and to grow from it.

With that in mind, let's dive right in. We were never kicked out of the Garden of Eden! Just before the end of the 20th Century, Pope John Paul II announced at some of his weekly audiences that neither heaven nor hell are places, but rather that they are states of consciousness. For those who have to see it with their own eyes, I direct you to the Vatican's website: (heaven – Wednesday Papal Audience 7/21/1999 at http://www.vatican.va/holy_father/john_paul_ii/audiences/1999/documents/hf_jp-ii_aud_21071999_en.html ; hell – Wednesday Papal Audience 7/28/1999 at http://www.vatican.va/holy_father/john_paul_ii/audiences/1999/documents/hf_jp-ii_aud_28071999_en.html .

Anyway, heaven and hell are states of consciousness, and the same is true for the Garden of Eden. Now, the Pope didn't say that; I said that. The Garden of Eden, too, is a state of consciousness. But that should be no big surprise. When we think about it, everything that is, has its reality in a state of consciousness. That's where we get sayings like, "one man's feast is another man's famine." So, the Garden of Eden, like heaven, and like hell, and, yes, even like the Kingdom of God, are all states of consciousness.

The Garden of Eden is a state of consciousness; it is not a place. As such, it is available to everyone at anytime. We can come and go, or we can stay. The choice has always been ours. But the key to regaining entrance to that garden state of consciousness is to accept and acknowledge our oneness with God.

So, in the stories of Genesis, where the early Hebrews record their take on the origin of "reality" as we know it, we have this story about a Garden. For some reason, in my youth I was under the impression that Adam and Eve just played in the Garden, but, in fact, if we read the story, we see that Adam is the gardener and Eve is his assistant. Here they are in the Garden of Eden and yet they have to work every day.

But we've all read the story, and we know that the serpent tempts Eve to eat the apple and when God finds out about it He curses them and drives them out of the jungle (oops, the garden). Now, if you've read your Bible and paid attention to what you read, you know that that is not the way it happened, though many ministers and many churches teach precisely that, with dire ramifications.

First, this is a story. It is not history. It is not the way things happened. It is not based upon actual events or actual people. It was never intended to be viewed in any of those ways other than as a story with underlying meanings. So what is the real story and what is its meaning?

Well adam-and-eve, not Adam and Eve, but adam&eve, are representative of each of us. They stand for the intellect and the feeling nature that is a part of you and me and every human who has ever passed this way. They are partners, and they tend to the garden in which they live and the garden provides them with all that they need. That's the way it is for each of us, even today. If we tend, take care of, the garden in which we live, it will provide for us.

All seems to be running smoothly until curiosity rears its head. We wonder if there could be more to reality than this garden in which we live. And isn't that the way life is? We can be in the middle of an incredible life and waste it away by dwelling on what we think is missing. Why do we do that? Well, one major reason is because we are like our creator and we need regular opportunities to express that creativity or else we implode. So we have an internal itch, a drive to discover, to experience, more.

As physical beings, we have a number of physical senses, or modes of perceiving reality. We're all familiar with sight, sound, taste, touch, and smell. But after awhile, the combination of all that data which is received by our physical senses begins to seduce us into thinking that the appearance is the reality, when, in truth, the reality is in the source, not in the appearance. But we concentrate on the appearance, and we get so comfortable in our relationship to the appearance that we gradually forget about the source. And the ego begins to worship itself instead of worshipping God.

Now, don't get me wrong. I'm not saying that the ego is bad. And I know that there are a lot of people out there who will disagree with me and claim that the ego is something that needs to be overcome before it overcomes us. And there's some truth to that, but not in a combative "take no prisoners" sense. The ego serves certain good purposes. It is an integral part of who we are on this plane of existence. BUT, it is not all there is. It is not God, although it sometimes thinks that it is. It tries to protect us, but it also tries to protect itself. AND, as long as we refuse to assume responsibility for our lives, our attitudes, and our consciousness, the ego will continue to try to successfully deceive us into believing that it is the boss.

It is from the "knowledge of good and evil" that the ego has ascended to power. We've said before that the great lie is in the belief that we are separate and apart from God. Judging by appearances, seeing things in the context of good and evil, creates the false appearance of separation. The appearance seems so much more real than the invisible truth from which it all springs that we lose our conscious connection to the source.

And when we do that, we suddenly feel very naked. We feel as if we must hide ourselves, for there appear to be powers out there that can harm us, that can cause us embarrassment if the truth of appearance about us be known. And as we judge ourselves inferior, we begin to doubt our right to continue to live in the garden. And so, by our attitudes and the ensuing actions, we banish ourselves from the garden ... and then we blame it all on God using the Genesis story for backup.

My dear friends, we never really left the garden. It has always been here. It's just that we have lost our ability to see it, to consciously experience it, because we are so caught up in the appearances. The garden is God's creation. Remember the story of creation? Time and time again it says, "And God saw that it was good." Then, finally, on the sixth day, Genesis 1:31, it says "And God saw everything that he had made, and, behold, it was very good."

It doesn't say that some was good and some was better. For hundreds and thousands of years people have sought the original "Garden of Eden," never realizing that they were always in it. No wonder they can't find it. Voltaire knew where it was when he wrote "Candide." Al Jolson knew where it was when he sang, "Back In Your Own Backyard." Lately I've been telling people that I have a picture of the "Garden of Eden." Then I show them the photograph taken by the Hubble Space Telescope Deep Field Project in which they discovered over 3,000 galaxies in a speck of space the size of a grain of sand (see the first chapter).

I think of these photos as the Garden of Eden for they demonstrate how God's creation is beyond our simple attempts at understanding it. We only discovered the existence of other galaxies a little over 100 years ago. Now we find over three trillion stars discovered down a twelve billion light year tunnel the size of a grain of sand.

Once at a Worship Service at Hillside Chapel and Truth Center in Atlanta, Georgia, Dr. Rocco Errico said that "the new Jerusalem is not a city, but rather is a community." He went on to say, however, that too many people would "rather have right doctrine than right action."

"Truth," he said, "is not a doctrine. Truth is the right action, at the right time, at the right place."

When we relearn how to do what's right, at the time that is right, and in the place that is right, we will rediscover our abode in the garden. It's high time we all made a concerted effort to be what God created us to be. The time is right for us to come home and reassume our place in the garden of life.

YOU ARE THE CHRIST

Our purpose, therefore, is to reveal the 'mystery hidden for ages:' that each of us is the Christ, the singularity, the totality of God in expression; that revelation comes through every choice we make, conscious or unconscious; all that we think, say, do, and feel is of God and is God.

YOU ARE THE CHRIST

In the previous chapter we talked about how we never left the Garden of Eden except in our ability to see it all around us. This time we want to return to an idea we first presented several chapters ago. We want to talk about the Christ and our relationship to that reality.

Our statement this time is: **Our purpose, therefore, is to reveal the "mystery hidden for ages:" that each of us is the Christ, the singularity, the totality of God in expression; that revelation comes through every choice we make, conscious or unconscious; all that we think, say, do, and feel is of God and is God.**

It is difficult for many people to comprehend, much less to accept, the divinity of each and every one of us. This is due largely to our conditioning. We live in a society which functions in contradiction to the truth of our being. But, I don't want you to take my word for it. Allow me to explain, through an example, what I mean by that statement about society.

In the United States, we have one phrase which appears on every single piece of coin and currency. It's a four word phrase. The phrase "e pluribus unum," which is Latin for "from many, one," appears on all the coins. "United States of America" appears on every coin, but the word "The" is tacked on the front end when the name of the country is printed on the currency. The unique four-word phrase which appears on every single coin **and** every single denomination of currency is, instead, **"In God We Trust."**

I think that at this point I can rest my case. I believe that most people know that by and large this is not true. In fact, the term I hear most often bandied about recently to describe this country is that it is a country governed by the rule of law. But when this country has more people per capita in jail than any other country on the planet, I wonder if we're talking about God's laws or we're talking about man's laws.

In God We Trust. Well, I question whether institutions trust in God. As for the individual human being, that's another matter. After all, before this was a "country of the rule of law," it was a country "of the people, by the people, and for the people." Of course that sentiment is not in an official document, but "only in a speech," as someone pointed out to me. Albeit the "speech" is Abraham Lincoln's "Gettysburg Address." I think that it is only people who can recognize the reality of a supreme being, a universal consciousness, a God in whom we can trust. I don't think that an institution can do that. After all, an institution, in and of itself, cannot think or feel. It has no soul. There's probably no evidence that its consciousness is anymore developed than that of a newt, if that.

Don't get me wrong here. I love this country. For whatever faults it may have, it has so much to recommend it that it is a beacon to hundreds of millions of people all over the world who desire to experience more in their lives.

But looking at institutions, themselves, the bottom line is that an institution cannot knowingly and realistically make the following claim: I am! And so, institutions, whether they be corporations, or governments, or churches, or whatever other type of humanly invented "organization," not one of them can say, "I am!" And, when you think about it, if one cannot say, "I am," then neither can one make the claim, "in God we trust." It is people, not institutions, which can trust in God. Personally, I believe that the reason "In God We Trust" is imprinted upon every piece of U.S. currency is because a large part of this country acts as though **money** is the God that we trust.

So, in a society joined at the hip to money and the market, we imprint "in God we trust" on all of our money and then pretend that the phrase has nothing to do with the God of money. If it weren't so sad, it would be laughable.

The "I am" that you are, and the "I am" that I am, is the embodiment of the "I am" that God is. For as far back as I can remember, I have been intrigued by that line from Exodus when Moses asked God, "Who shall I say has sent me." "I am that I am" was the reply in the standard King James vernacular.

If "I am" is who sent Moses to the people with the law, and we are created in that image and after that likeness, then that "I am" is the active, creative presence of God expressing through us. And it expresses in whatever way we choose, for we have been given the freedom of choice. Free will. I am ... what? I am tired? I am happy? I am lonely? I am healthy? We think the thought. We speak the word. Reality manifests.

New Thought teaches the power in the declaration of denials and affirmations. In other words, the thought or spoken thought, or word has power. And the most powerful of the words, the most creative of all the words, the most dynamic of all thoughts are those that are driven by the vibration of "I am." (See Chapter Four)

In many Christian churches it is taught that we are not to take the Lord's name in vain. And that is interpreted to mean statements like, "God damn," or "Jesus H Christ." But if God told Moses that it is "I am who sends you," and that "I am" is "I am that I am," then I think we should be a lot more concerned about the words which we use in conjunction with "I am." In fact, I think that, once knowing what I've just shared, we'd be downright stupid if we attached any negative, limiting thoughts or words to our use of the powerful "I am."

Now, what does all of this have to do with the current statement? Well, that "I am" that God is, expressing in a multitude of ways as the "I am" that I am, and the "I am" that you are, and the infinity of God's creation being "I am," is the activity which we call the Christ. And, in our infinite uniqueness, it is the singularity which each of us is. I feel here like shouting like the old time preacher, "Glory, hallelujah!"

The mystery which Paul talks about in his letter to the Colossians owes its mystery to the lack of our realization of our I amness, and what that means. I say that you are divine I am, and there are Christian preachers who will cry, "Blasphemer." The same charge was made against Jesus in his own day by the Pharisees, those who believed in the strict letter of the law. People today professing to be doing the work of Jesus still accuse those who practice his teachings of being in contradiction to "God's laws." They are condemned and accused of being in opposition to the very teachings which they claim to believe and practice. But friends, it doesn't matter what anyone else says. It doesn't matter what credentials they may have. What is that to thee? You are a child of God. Ask God, right here, right now, what is right. Within yourself, in your gut, you know, right this very moment, that I speak the truth. "The mystery hidden for ages …. Christ in you, your hope of glory." In you. Right now. Your hope. Your experience of glory.

Every one of us, no matter what path we have trod, is on the path to ultimately discovering who and what we are at the deepest levels of our being. And it may take a little while or it may take a long time for one to realize the truth about themselves, and that's all right. You know, when one looks at the Deep Field pictures taken by the Hubble Space Telescope, what we see is the light from events which took place billions of years ago. It took that long for the light which registered that picture to get to the Hubble. The Hubble Deep Field pictures are pictures of billions of years of history. When we look at it on that scale, it can make what seems "important" to us appear to be pretty puny. And yet. And yet. As James Michener put it so aptly in his novel, "Space," what little we have done "has gotten us to where we are, and that's not insignificant." In fact it is very profound.

When we take the time to "stop and smell the roses," as they used to say, it all can become extremely profound. Right here. Right now. This is not a promise of some future date. God's promises are right here, right now, just waiting for us to awaken from the sleep of judging merely by appearances. Jesus brought us the message that the Kingdom of God is at hand. Look at your hand. Right now. Where is it? It is right here. It is right now. And so it is with the Kingdom of God. It quietly, patiently awaits our acknowledgment and acceptance of it. I feel sometimes like screaming, as Jim Morrison did in the beginning of the "Celebration of the Lizard," "Wake up!" You know, Jesus said it. "Awake, thou that sleepest." We have eyes, yet we do not see. We have ears, yet we do not hear. "Wake up!"

Once, while downloading some songs from Napster, I got into a place where I discovered that there are a lot of versions of the song, "Amazing Grace." I began downloading them. I've been listening to that song as I originally prepared much of this chapter. Amazing Grace. I now have over 300 different versions of that song on my computer. Amazing Grace. How sweet the sound that touched a soul like me. I once was lost, but now I'm found. Was blind, but now I see. If you know the story of how that song came to be written, think about it again. It was written by the captain of a slave ship who had a profound realization which caused him to turn his ship around, mid-ocean, and set off in a new direction with his life. It's a song of hope, not for the future, but for right now. Anyone can turn around, any time. And now is the best time there is, because now is the only time we have.

One Sunday, John Strickland, the Senior Minister at Atlanta Unity, talked about the story of Jacob and how he was a liar and a deceiver, and how his life was filled with the lies and deceit of others. But finally one day he decided to stop running, to turn around, to find himself, to confront himself, and to be himself, without trying any longer to deceive others. And he wrestled all night, but he refused to give up until he received a blessing. And he prevailed. He confronted his past. And the way was made clear. And that very day he became Israel, the prince of God.

Today can be your day. Any day can be your day to turn from what you have been, to embrace what you can be. When I heard what John Strickland said, I decided, once again, like Jacob, to turn over a new leaf and begin again. This is the ongoing power of the I am that we are. We can reinvent ourselves anytime we choose.

Today I am love. I am life. I am health. I am abundance. I am peace. I am joy. I am strength. I am prosperity. I am wisdom. I am enthusiasm. I am happy. I am good judgment. I am understanding. I am power. I am will. I am. I am spirit, and I am grateful.

I declare for you that this is a blessed day and I rejoice with you as you let your Christ light shine. You are special. I recognize your uniqueness, and I truly love you.

When I first wrote this book, I inserted a half dozen pages here of extensive quotes from Charles Fillmore's *"The Metaphysical Bible Dictionary."* I examined Charles' metaphysical analyses of the words "Christ," "Jehovah," "Messiah" and "I Am." I invite the reader to contemplate those writings if they desire a deeper understanding of what these related terms mean (i.e. Buy The Book). For those who know little or nothing about Charles Fillmore, or who are curious what this talk of "metaphysics" is all about, these quotes from Fillmore's magnum opus provide an excellent window of insight into both subjects. For now, however, I will simply point out here what we can glean in a nutshell from these writings.

Christ is man as created by God. The result of a Divine Idea. Furthermore, Jesus is an individual expression of that Divine Creation. He is revered through the ages because of his expression of that Divine Idea, the Christ.

Jehovah, JHVH in Hebrew, is often translated "Lord" and means "the ever living male-and-female principle. The word "Christ" appears nowhere in the Old Testament. So we might think of Jehovah as an Old Testament equivalent of the New Testament "Christ."

The word "Messiah," which is often juxtaposed with the word "Christ" means the anointed one, "baptized of the Holy Spirit." It is endowed with a special mission of illumination and enlightenment.

This all brings us to "I Am," the name of God as given to, or perceived by, Moses. This is a term that signifies infinite eternity. Charles Fillmore says, "I AM is God's name in man; it is Jehovah, the indwelling Christ, the true spiritual man whom God made in his image and likeness." I would add that the beliefs that we attach to these words, "I Am," are the portal through which God expresses itself in us.

So what this all means is that we are co-creators through the I AM because the I AM is at the core of our being. It is who we actually are. That voice which talked to Moses from the burning bush is the same voice that speaks through you and me as a multitude of ideas, feelings, actions, and perceptions.

When Deepak Chopra tells us that we are a field of all possibilities, that is what I AM is, all possibilities existing in a field of potentiality. But what brings that potentiality into expression? It is your will and mine.

All possibilities exist. The link from the field of possibility to the appearance of what we call reality is in the observer, the experiencer, the I am. The story of ongoing creation. "I-am---I-was---I-will-be because I-am---I-was---I-will-be the power to be eternally I."

All time is now. I am, I was, and I will be is all here and now. It's all just a matter of different perspectives.

Reality is composed of an infinite number of parallel universes. We choose which of those infinite universes we live in from moment to moment by the thoughts we think, the feelings we have, the perceptions which we hold dear.

Reality is not linear; it's omni-directional. All possibilities are available to each and every one of us. It is always up to us as to which we choose. And how do we do that? Well, that's why we're here, to discover who and what we are and how to go about making the best use of our capabilities.

The complete picture is beyond our understanding and our total communication. It must be that way because we must have the motivation and the drive to allow the I AM to manifest through us in eventual ultimate totality.

This, then, is what Jesus came to teach us and what I believe Unity continues to teach, that we are children of God, created in God's image and after God's likeness, that we are therefore heirs to all good and the channels for God's substance to come into manifestation. We are the Christ.

Our purpose, therefore, as we will be detailing with our final statement, next chapter, is to reveal the "mystery hidden for ages:" that each of us is the Christ, the singularity, the totality of God in expression; that revelation comes through every choice we make, conscious or unconscious; all that we think, say, do, and feel is of God and is God.

I AM the Christ, child of the living God. I am not flesh and blood; I AM Spirit.

OUR PURPOSE IS TO BE

Our purpose is expressed through apprehending and comprehending the beauty of the singularity and striving to consciously participate with it at every level of our being.

OUR PURPOSE IS TO BE

By our fruits are we all known.

For the past nine chapters, we've been looking at "What We Believe That Makes Us Different." That title came about as a result of a lifetime of my being questioned and confronted by people whose alleged desire to understand what I believe, where spiritual matters are concerned, masked an effort to undermine those beliefs and supplant them with their own views. It's like they were trying to religionize my spirit. I would look at books which claimed that Unity is a cult and I would read the quotes that they would use from Unity writings and then scratch my head, wondering why anyone would find reason to disagree with Unity's viewpoint.

I eventually came to understand that this New Thought Movement, which began over 100 years ago as an attempt to shed the excessive baggage of doctrine, dogma, form, and ritual which had come to obscure, like plaque on teeth, the basic teachings of Jesus and other master teachers, was still having to coexist in a world where outmoded doctrines had so infiltrated the culture that one often felt like an outsider for being able to see beyond the doctrinal obscurity. (Whew, that was a mouthful.) Following one particularly pointed attempt at undermining my beliefs, I realized that I was reacting to my inquisitor more than I wished. Examining my response, and looking for a reason why this situation agitated me as much as it did, I realized that I was still uncomfortable not only with knowing what I believed, but also with being able to discern how it differed from the beliefs of the more fundamentalist people in our society. It was obviously time to get grounded once again. So I asked myself, "What is it that we believe that makes us so different?" The result has become this book on ten orderly statements.

In the previous chapter we talked about our true nature. We are, at our core, spiritual beings. At present we are spiritual beings expressing through physical bodies. When those bodies are discarded as no longer useful, we will still be spiritual beings. We always have been spiritual beings and we always will be spiritual beings. Because we are spiritual beings in a matrix of unlimited, infinite possibilities, redundancy is unnecessary. Each of us, therefore, is absolutely, totally unique: a singularity, so to speak. The singularity that you are is the way in which you allow the Christ, spirit consciousness, to express through you.

Once we understand that perspective about our true nature, we must then revisit the question which has intrigued humanity throughout its history, "What's our purpose for being?" Thus, our tenth and final statement in this series is: **Our purpose is expressed through apprehending and comprehending the beauty of the singularity and striving to consciously participate with it at every level of our being.**

Very few people have any real grasp upon the purpose for their existence. The basic reason for that is that we see ourselves backwards from reality. What I mean by that is that we think of ourselves in reference to.

It's similar to what we talk about when we think of the flow of the universe. The universe flows from Being to Doing to Having. This is no different from what Unity teaches when we talk about Mind, Idea and Expression.

With Mind, Idea, and Expression, we understand that Ideas stem from Mind and cause or result in Expression. That's a flow that we can readily relate to. We understand that Expression does not create Ideas which then cause the existence of Mind. That concept sounds blatantly silly. And yet, when it comes to the flow of the universe, we blithely traipse along living our lives backwards without a second thought and without considering the foolishness of what we're doing. Life does not flow from Having to Doing to Being, yet that's how most people are trying to live their lives. That's because we have spent our lives concentrating upon the expression instead of upon the source, the effects instead of the cause.

Jesus came to change all of that, to give us a different perspective. A different perspective. Sometimes I think that would be just as good a name for my ministry. Instead of calling it Practical Truth Ministry we could just call it A Different Perspective Ministry. That would work well because to know and understand the Truths that Jesus and other enlightened individuals have shared with us is a different perspective from the ways in which most people live their lives.

How do I know that? By merely looking at the expressions around me. This world in which we live, this world which most people think of as reality, is expression. It is result. It is not source. It is not cause. It has no power. It is just a thing which has come about because of the working of the true reality.

What is that true reality? It's what we've been talking about throughout this book. It is what we endeavor to live in our lives. It is the Truth in Practical Truth. It is the basic foundation of Jesus' teaching. Even an expression junkie like Paul was able to glimpse the true reality when he said, "Christ in you, the hope of glory."

True reality is process. It is not thing. Some people, in their quest for the Truth, find their way back to the Source, to Mind, to Being, and they are so astonished by the difference of the ideas and the feelings generated by this discovery in comparison to the Result, the Expression, the Having, the Appearance, that they go, "Aha, I have found it!" and they devote their life to getting involved in that primal cause experience.

If they are not careful, however, they get so sucked in to that reality of the source that they end up "so heavenly minded that they are no earthly good." We have all seen this result in some Eastern religious cultures. We often see this happening in relationships. One party in a relationship glimpses a different perspective, says, "Aha, I've found it," and dumps the other party if they don't "see it" also.

Now, understand here, I'm not condemning that approach. I'm merely observing and commenting. It's like if somebody were trying to open a door that says "pull" by pushing on it. For me to observe what others are doing and to comment on it is not a judgment of their actions. In fact, if I speculate on the possible results of their actions, even that is not a judgment upon them, merely an observation upon their actions and where those actions may take them.

We sometimes forget this when we are thinking and talking and feeling about ourselves and about others. We see the results of our actions as who we are. But if we go to the other end of the spectrum and see the source of our actions as who we are, then I don't see that as being any different in its ultimate results. It's merely a matter of perspective. But it's not really the Truth, not the whole Truth.

Sometimes it is very difficult to decide just what to say when I speak on a Sunday morning, or in a class, and how to say it because our language is so limiting. All languages have their limitations, but English sometimes seems to have more limitations than other languages. That's probably because English, being Western, is into efficiency, and efficiency can strangle the fullness, stripping it to the bare bones. Poetry is an effort to combat that overemphasis upon efficiency. Be that as it may, I'm having difficulty here with some of the terms which I am using.

For instance, the word "Being". That word can be either a noun or a verb. It can be either thing or action. I was listening to Alan Watts recently and he was talking about how our language is constructed in such a way that we demand that every verb have a noun, a subject, an object, a thing. He says that Chinese is not like that, and that, therefore, it is possible in Chinese to say just as much in half the time.

His point here is that in our Western perspective, thing, expression, result is of the utmost importance. And so when I use the word "Being" I'm always aware that it can be interpreted by others as either action or thing. And even then, I don't feel truly comfortable referring to Being as thing. And yet when we speak of "a Being" we are speaking in terms of thing.

In our Flow of the Universe analogy, Being appears as thing, and yet the entire flow itself, from Being through Doing to Having, can be called Being. And that is not "thing" but rather "process." So, in our tenth statement, considering our purpose of being, we need to be aware that we are talking about process.

This is a most important consideration for us, for the success of our quest for understanding who and what we are hinges upon our understanding that it is process that is the ultimate truth rather than any of the aspects of process. Note here that I don't speak of "the process" but instead of "process." The word "the" implies thingdom. I'm not talking about thing. I'm talking about flow, and that's because that's what it is really all about. It's not the source, or the expression, or even the process of one becoming the other, but the flow of all of it that is important.

Consider again our statement: **Our purpose is expressed through apprehending and comprehending the beauty of the singularity and striving to consciously participate with it at every level of our being.**

Our purpose of being, our reason, the truth of who we really are

...is expressed, is brought to our fuller comprehension and understanding

...through apprehending and comprehending, through becoming more fully cognizant

...of the beauty of the singularity, of the reality of the entire unique process that we are, rather than as aspects of that process

...and striving to consciously participate, dedicating our lives, our efforts, our concentration, and our actions to bringing an awareness of that process of flow into our full conscious awareness in all of its aspects

...and doing this at every level of our being, aware that we are, in truth, infinite possibility.

We live in a world of appearance. The appearance is so overwhelming for most of us, because we have so many ways of perceiving it, through our sight, through sounds, through touch, through smells, through tastes, through feelings, through the power of our concentration, through the amplification of our imagination, and through the action of our brains in constantly, relentlessly processing all of this data of appearance, that we have gotten lost in thinking that the appearance is reality.

But that's merely a perspective.

Eric Butterworth quoted Charles Fillmore as saying that people would come to him all of the time asking him to pray with them to change their marriage, or their job, or their health, or their finances, or their habits, or their children, or their parents. But, he said, they never would ask him to help them by praying to change the only thing that anyone **can** change - their minds.

Hear that loud and clear. The only thing you can change is your mind. The only thing you can change is your perspective. The only thing you can change is what you decide to concentrate upon, what you decide to believe.

Think back to Unity's teaching of Mind, Idea, and Expression. Fillmore tells us that capital M Mind is synonymous with Spirit. This is God. Mind generates Ideas resulting in Expression. That Mind is all there is. All else springs from that Source.

You have access to that Mind. That's because you are that Mind. If that Mind is all there is, then you cannot be anything other than that Mind. The reality is Mind.

In a nutshell, our purpose for being is to be. Don't make the mistake here of thinking that "just being" means "just surviving." If we look around at this infinite universe of unlimited possibilities in which we are experiencing, although mere survival might appear at first blush to be a way of life or an end in and of itself, if we step back and observe the larger picture, we see that life is a process of constant change, resulting in continuous growth. Although that growth may go through seasonal changes, the still larger picture reveals that the growth continues expansively, regardless of the temporary appearances. That's why chaos theory ultimately results in exquisitely unpredictable order.

Remember that every major breakthrough in civilization all but destroys the society from which it springs. We sometimes hear people talk of the "fall of the Roman Empire" and use the images of the ancient Roman collapse to condemn contemporary events. But, although the Roman Empire did come to an end, as such, it was succeeded by empires more grand than the Romans ever could have imagined.

We see this kind of change taking place in our world today. Many of us find the change uncomfortable. We long for the security of the past as we remember it. But, as Thomas Wolfe said, "you can't go home again." And the reason is that the past no longer exists for us except in memory. The only thing that exists in experience for us is the present, and it is speeding towards the future. Tomorrow, today will be the past. And while we can make it a memorable past, we can also choose to make of it a past which looks to the future, rather than being self-absorbed.

In order for this to happen, two things are absolutely necessary. First, we must be aware of who we are. And secondly, we must act upon that awareness. And that's precisely what God created us to do: to become self-aware and to act from that self awareness. We must discover and comprehend the truth of our being. Step beyond the limited belief in mere appearance and discover your source, that wellspring from which flows unlimited potential and possibility.

What we have shared here in the past several chapters is an orderly process of awareness in which we start with the premise that God is all there is and finally arrive at the realization that our purpose for being is to allow God to express more fully through our lives. It is imperative that a diligent effort be made to achieve this awareness and experience. We are living in a time and at a place where we are being bombarded thousands of times each day by temptations to put the full realization of who and what we are aside and to concentrate on channeling our interest, energy, and efforts into supporting someone else's appearance-driven construct. Our sense of value of our own self-worth is often eroded. If it returns at all, it usually does with a frustrating sense of too little, too late.

I could weave a very convincing and depressing scenario detailing how our present society has negatively impacted the quality of our lives and seduced millions of people into a lifetime in which they, themselves, are no longer in control. But instead I'll merely summarize with an example of how wrapped up we are in the race of the rat.

Some friends have just retired. A couple, both retiring from jobs at relatively the same time. They were recently over for dinner and I asked them both, "do you find yourself wondering where you ever found the time to have a job?" They both concurred, wholeheartedly.

Personally, I have experienced both extremes. I had a period in my life when I applied for 600 jobs over a 13 month period before I finally got a job offer and was hired. At the other extreme, I've had a time in my life when I was sufficiently well-off financially that I could do what I wished, when I wished, with whom I wished, and in the way that I wished. And I've had a multitude of experiences between those two opposite lifestyles. As a result, based upon personal experience, I know what it is like to live in this society across the economic spectrum. Why do I look at things in terms of economics? Because that's the driving force of the society which we have created. That's right. The society which "we" have created. It revolves around the bottom line, the return on investment, the latest market quotes. Hail, Caesar.

But I also know that there are other realities out there, with millions of participants, which forego the entrapments which our society sets for us. I saw some Ram Dass audio files on Napster one night. In the titles, one said something like, "materialism is a trap." But the very next title said, "Anti-materialism is a trap." And that's absolutely true. As long as we support it or fight it, we give it life and prolong it. What we want to do is to surpass it, to transcend it. As the Sufi poet Rumi said, "Out beyond right-doing and wrong-doing, there is a field. I'll meet you there." We're striving to meet in that field.

My next book, which I'm already working on, will be a cornucopia of perspectives on how to coexist with the changes which are so rapidly taking place in the world today. It will be a more secular follow-up to this volume. It promises to be full of incredibly unique possibilities and perspectives, and all connected with the principles we have dealt with here.

At your very core, as Deepak Chopra says, you are a field of all possibilities. Every single day, when you awake, you begin "again" to choose how you will allow that field to express in and through your life. Many people think that God's reality is somehow devoid of that daily awakening of "again," but that's where the core of excitement lies. Again. Every day is a new beginning. Like they used to say several decades ago, "today is the first day of the rest of your life." Although it may have gotten to where it sounded trite, nevertheless, that is our reality here and now. I would modify it to say that each and every moment is a new beginning. Each and every choice is a new beginning. Will the next one be a choice leading to a new beginning that is in line with the truth of our nature and the core of our deeper image of ourselves, or will the next moment be a choice leading to more of the same. Well, it doesn't really matter. That moment has already passed into the past. Next!

Our purpose for being is to Be. To Be. Not to judge. To Be. Not to seek guidance from appearance. To Be. Our purpose for being is to Be.

What can we be? The possibilities are infinitely endless. We are not just the expression of God, we are also the channels of that expression, we are also that very God. It is all one. It is all a flow. It is all a process.

Let's become still as I offer a prayer.

Beloved, Source of all, ongoing, ever changing, evolutionary process, we release our hold on the seeming reality of appearance and acknowledge the truth of who and what we are.

We believe that God is all there is; absolute, total, without exception.

God is all good, therefore everything that is, is good.

There is no evil; evil is actually a denial of the truth that there is no evil; evil's only existence rests in one's belief in its existence; therefore evil is the great lie of a belief in separation from God.

We are created in the image and after the likeness of God; the word for that creation is the Christ; it is the core of every one of us, without exception; we therefore cannot be separate from God, for we are totally God in expression.

What God does is to express itself; since God is all there is, then this expression is multitudinously infinite.

As an expression of God, each of us is unique, a singularity; Jesus is a unique expression of God; you are a unique expression of God; everyone and everything is a unique expression of God; no one individual expression is better or worse than any other expression; each is a singularity; each is absolutely, totally, uniquely, singularly, exquisitely, fully God in expression.

To question or doubt the divinity of our singularity is the ultimate sin of denial; it is denying the existence of, and the full and complete expression of, God.

Our belief in separation from God causes us to lose sight of the Garden of Eden in which we reside; the garden is the full and total infinite expression of God.

Our purpose, therefore, is to reveal the "mystery hidden for ages:" that each of us is the Christ, the singularity, the totality of God in expression; that revelation comes through every choice we make, conscious or unconscious; all that we think, say, do, and feel is of God and is God.

Our purpose is expressed through apprehending and comprehending the beauty of the singularity and striving to consciously participate with it at every level of our being.

We do give thanks that it is so. Amen.

My prayer for you, dear friend, is that your passion for the singularity that you are gets fanned into a flame of new beginnings that allows for a greatly enhanced life in which you discover and experience your deeper purpose for being. You have my most profound blessings upon your exquisite journey of discovery.

Ten Statements

First: God is all there is; absolute, total, without exception.

Second: God is all good, therefore everything that is is good.

Third: There is no evil; evil is actually a denial of the truth that there is no evil; evil's only existence rests in one's belief in its existence; therefore evil is the great lie of a belief in separation from God.

Fourth: We are created in the image and after the likeness of God; the word for that creation is the Christ; it is the core of every one of us, without exception; we therefore cannot be separate from God, for we are totally God in expression.

Fifth: What God does is to express itself; since God is all there is, then this expression is multitudinously infinite.

Sixth: As an expression of God, each of us is unique, a singularity; Jesus is a unique expression of God; you are a unique expression of God; everyone and everything is a unique expression of God; no one individual expression is better or worse than any other expression; each is a singularity; each is absolutely, totally, uniquely, singularly, exquisitely, fully God in expression.

Seventh: To question or doubt the divinity of our singularity is the ultimate sin of denial; it is denying the existence of, and the full and complete expression of, God.

Eighth: Our belief in separation from God causes us to lose sight of the Garden of Eden in which we reside; the garden is the full and total infinite expression of God.

Ninth: Our purpose, therefore, is to reveal the "mystery hidden for ages:" that each of us is the Christ, the singularity, the totality of God in expression; that revelation comes through every choice we make, conscious or unconscious; all that we think, say, do, and feel is of God and is God.

Tenth: Our purpose is expressed through apprehending and comprehending the beauty of the singularity and striving to consciously participate with it at every level of our being.

About The Author

Rev. Charles DeTurk is the son of a freelance entertainer and a Unity minister. He and his brother Larry spent part of their early years entertaining on stage, radio and television (and occasionally in nightclubs where their father worked).

Charles grew up in Unity, was elected International Youth of Unity President in 1964, and lived at Unity School of Christianity, working in Silent Unity and in the Youth Department of the Field Department.

Although his intention, from his teens, was to be a minister, he wasn't ordained until he was 50, spending the intervening years in a variety of pursuits that has given him an extremely wide and varied background of experience and the freedom to be open to new ideas and different, often unique, perspectives. He has published an alternative paper, worked at a number of Fortune 500 companies, universities, and state and federal government agencies, run a computer department, and been a checkout clerk in an eclectic New Mexico village market.

Charles lives in Georgia with his wife Sherri, and devotes a good deal of his time to writing, speaking, teaching, and enjoying the glory of grandchildren. He also has quite an extensive collection of writings on a number of blogs that he attempts to maintain on the Internet.

Rev. DeTurk is available for speaking and teaching engagements. Email: RevDeTurk@yahoo.com or Practical Truth, P.O. Box 1763, Decatur, GA 30031

Made in the USA
Charleston, SC
25 January 2011